P9-DJV-140

Phoning Home

PHONING

The University of South Carolina Press

HOME ESSAYS

Jacob M. Appel

© 2014 University of South Carolina

Published by the University of South Carolina Press
Columbia, South Carolina 29208

www.sc.edu/uscpress

Manufactured in the United States of America

23 22 21 20 19 18 17 16 15 14   11 10 9 8 7 6 5 4 3 2

Library of Congress Cataloging-in-Publication Data

Appel, Jacob M., 1973–
   Phoning home : essays / Jacob M. Appel.
      pages cm
   ISBN 978-1-61117-371-0 (hardback)—ISBN 978-1-61117-372-7 (ebook)
      1. Appel, Jacob M., 1973– 2. Appel, Jacob M., 1973—Family.
   3. Physicians—United States—Biography. 4. Lawyers—United States—
   Biography. 5. Bioethicists—United States—Biography. I. Title.
   CT275.A768A3 2014
   610.92—dc23
   [B]   2013042682

For Rosalie

Contents

Acknowledgments

The essays in this volume previously appeared in the following periodicals: "Phoning Home" in *Massachusetts Review* (March 2007), "Two Cats, Fat and Thin" in *Briar Cliff Review* (2008), "Mr. Odd and Mr. Even" in *Georgetown Review* (April 2009), "The Man Who Was Not My Grandfather" in *Midstream* (Winter 2012), "Caesura—Antwerp, 1938" in *Tiferet* (March 2013), "An Absence of Jell-O" in *Southwest Review* (Spring 2011), "She Loves Me Not" in *Passages North* (Winter/Spring 2006), "Opting Out" in *North Dakota Quarterly* (Fall 2009), "Charming and Devoted" in *Alligator Juniper* (January 2010), "Livery" in *Southeast Review* (Winter/Spring 2012), "Sudden Death—A Eulogy," in *Kenyon Review* (2013), "Our Incredible Shrinking Discourse" in *CutBank* (Spring 2010), and "Divided Expectations" in *Chattahoochee Review* (Spring 2012).

Phoning Home

During the summer following my seventh birthday, my parents began receiving prank telephone calls from an anonymous source. These calls ranged in frequency from once in an afternoon to many times in an hour, and the barrage lasted for several months, until eventually my parents changed their phone number—to an unlisted line that they still give out on only a selective basis. After that the calls stopped abruptly. Never again did we hear from the mysterious "crank caller" who had disturbed our dinners so effectively in those early days of the Reagan administration. Nor did my parents ever learn his identity, despite a dogged police trace. In the years before caller ID and computerized tracking, our tormenter appeared to know precisely how long he could stay on the line until the authorities trailed him to his lair. Mom and Dad harbored suspicions, of course. Or at least Mom did. She blamed my father's estranged brother, a rather peculiar and troubled man who had disappeared from the lives of his own parents and siblings shortly after my birth and then reappeared eleven years later without offering any explanation. Why my uncle would bother to phone us incessantly, if he did not wish to communicate with us, has never been entirely clear to me—it seems to me that, since he wasn't on speaking terms with my father and had actually hung up angrily when my grandfather called him, my uncle would have been the last person likely to contact us by phone—but at the time my mother found considerable comfort in blaming her absent brother-in-law. I suppose being the target of an irksome relative is far more heartening than being stalked by some unknown sex fiend or hate group.

Our caller's modus operandi lacked much of the panache of more celebrated cranks. He neither panted nor grunted suggestively. He didn't ask after men named Al Coholic and Jacques Strappe or inquire if our refrigerator was running and then urge us to chase after it. Not once did he dish out a slur, level a threat, or laugh maniacally. The man merely waited for one of my parents to answer our rotary phones—either the olive-green wall console in the kitchen or the canary-yellow extension in the master bedroom, both rented from Ma Bell for thirty-five dollars a month—and he hung up. My father's shouts into the receiver were invariably greeted by a long interval of silence and then a polite click. If my mother happened to answer the phone—and she did so with less and less frequency —she tried to reason with those intervals of silence, the same sort of futile negotiations she often conducted in attempting to lure our pet rabbit up a staircase. When under heavy stress, my mother has a voice that could tarnish copper. I can still hear her pointing out the flaws in the caller's methodology, as though it were a mathematical problem: "You wouldn't be calling us if you didn't want something. But if you don't tell us what you want, we won't know what it is. And if we don't know what it is, we can't give it to you. So why are you calling us? Explain yourself, please." Did my mother really expect an answer? Or was this merely her version of repeating "hello" into a dial tone? All I can say for certain is that she didn't learn our caller's motives.

I still have no idea what made this creature tick—what drove him to torment an otherwise inconsequential suburban family who had done him no harm. And if I don't know, I imagine nobody will ever know. Because I was him.

I am now thirty-two years old, and, for better or worse, people consistently turn to me when they want to share their secrets. Sometimes I flatter myself into believing that this reflects esteem for my discretion and empathy—or a misplaced confidence that as a writer I am somehow above the fray of judgment. Often, of course, people trust me because they think I also harbor deep secrets of my own . . . and they'll even tell me so, readily, as did one colleague, who took the liberty of informing me that he knew he could confide in me because I was so obviously a closeted homosexual. I'm not sure what he meant by this declaration—maybe that if I betrayed his confidence, he'd attempt to expose me—but I endured his confessions without bothering to disabuse him of his premises. Sometimes people trust me merely because I am there. (As Woody Allen says, 99 percent of life is showing up.) But if that is the case, I can't help concluding that there must be many others like me, an entire infantry of ad-hoc confessors, each roaming the earth with his or her own trove of secrets. All one must do, as Polonius warns Laertes, is "give every man thine ear but few thy voice," and the transgressions of humanity are yours to wallow in. Nor are these the plagiaristic, selectively edited confessions that Nick Carraway complains of in the opening pages of *The Great Gatsby.* At the least, in my experience, many people lead lives governed by deceits of Shakespearean dimensions—deceits which they prove all too willing to share, over a beer or a milkshake, in every last lurid and lamentable detail.

Although I am no longer shocked by any particular confession—whether to infidelity or criminality or even adult illiteracy—I do remain continually amazed at how little I know about the people closest to me. This is not meant as an epistemological observation about the inability of human beings to transcend that great divide between self and other. I am beyond the question of whether my "yellow" is the same as my neighbor's "yellow," whether basic emotions such as love and grief can ever be transcendent. I no longer care. So when I say that I don't know about the people around me, what I mean is that, on multiple occasions, a friend or coworker has chosen to keep me ignorant of crucial facts regarding background, identity, or lifestyle. The sad part is that it is usually the secrecy, rather than the underlying secret, that I find hardest to accept. Although I would never have abandoned these individuals on account of their lapses—everything from forging credentials to seducing students—the fact that they weren't the scrupulous academics or faithful spouses I'd previously thought them somehow requires a rethinking of the entire relationship. It also makes you wonder what secrets other people haven't told you. Not that you are entirely without blame, particularly when you are the "crank caller" who terrorized 117 Carthage Road from June to August 1981.

The summer I made such effective use of the telephone, my parents were about the same age as I am now. This was before my mother's breakdown, before my father became nephrologist to the stars. We lived in a split-level ranch house that my parents had purchased from the owner of the Pechter Bread Company, in its heyday the biggest name in Jewish rye. (Mr. Pechter dropped by one afternoon to retrieve some liquor bottles he'd stored in the cellar, and I still remember my disappointment that he didn't wear a puffy chef's hat or carry a rolling pin.) There was a garden out back where my father planted the Passover horseradish that our family transported from address to address like a treasured heirloom, and also beds of *polygonum,* a pink wildflower that my younger brother once consumed in large enough quantities to spark a panicked phone call to Poison Control. My mother's stepmother— Grandma Ida—came to live with us. She brought with her a telephone line of her own, and also an inlaid rosewood telephone table and a pocket-sized address book in which the phone exchanges were still written in letters, rather than numbers. In short, in the months leading up to my calling spree, we were just another run-of-the-mill middle-class family.

Were we happy? I'd like to say yes. I have strong, positive memories from the period: outings to the zoo and the botanical gardens, apple-picking expeditions, constructing intricate dioramas from Christmas tree bulbs. Once, I accompanied my grandmother to the supermarket, and we took part in a focus group that introduced kiwi fruit to American audiences. On another occasion, my father roasted chestnuts without first slicing air holes, bombarding our kitchen with a phalanx of steaming projectiles—and we spent days knocking the remnants off the ceiling with a broom handle. Each of these memories, discrete droplets, suggests happiness. Or at least joy. For my parents were the sort of people who sought joy, not the type who contemplated happiness.

Maybe it is better to say that we seemed happy. Even in hindsight, it's impossible to know for sure: who can tell what unexpected love letters or drug paraphernalia or diary confessions will emerge someday when we clean out my parents' closets. Not that I have any evidence or suspicion that they're holding out on me—far from it. But they probably look at me and think the same. Moreover, the statistics on the prevalence of dishonesty in all of its various guises are truly damning. As Professor Kingsfield says in *The Paper Chase:* "Look to the right of you, look to the left of you. . . ."

What's most remarkable about my career as a deranged lunatic is that it started and stopped at the age of seven, an isolated incident without precursor or follow-up. I imagine that—had I been caught—I'd have been remitted to a team of child psychiatrists to have my brain poked and prodded until they uprooted the source of my madness. If I were left to my own devices, these authorities would have assured my desperate parents, I'd have amounted to no good. The boy who crank calls his family becomes the adolescent who vandalizes synagogues and grows into the adult who snatches purses from senior citizens, etc. As it turned out, none of that came to pass. No shrinks. No juvenile delinquency. No overt sign of sociopathy. In fact, I now teach courses in law and ethics to undergraduates. My second-grade indiscretions notwithstanding, my superego could out arm-wrestle my id with one hand tied behind its back.

Despite all the experts' claims about troubled children growing into troubled adults—and I've explored the literature extensively—I think I've overcome this episode relatively unscathed. I certainly do not flee from my secret like Conrad's Lord Jim or inflict it on others in the manner of Dickens's Miss Havisham. I'm confident that no authority on telephone stalkers could pick my psychological profile out of a lineup. And, just so the record is entirely clear, I've never hung up on someone again. I don't even hang up on answering machines or telemarketers. Maybe I feel guilty. Or maybe I've surpassed my quota. (If I were so inclined, I might develop a mercantilist theory of hang-ups, in which a limited number must supply the entire world—but I am not so inclined.) Whatever the case, I rarely think about my days as a crank. When I do, it is usually with complete befuddlement: what possesses a seven-year-old to take up phone terror? Of course, that younger me is utterly inaccessible. I no longer understand what causes a seven-year-old to do anything at all.

I don't actually remember making the first call. It might have been inconsequential at the moment, a child's exploration gone awry. (Only months earlier, when my aunt had phoned from Florida, I'd naively answered her questions by nodding and shaking my head.) What I do recall are the great lengths I went to in order to conceal and perpetuate my antics. My initial method of attack was quite straightforward: I waited until my grandmother left her room and then called my parents from her telephone. But I wasn't above additional maneuvers to divert suspicion—such as leaving my grandmother's phone right after dialing and then running downstairs to watch my mother negotiating with the silent line. Or, when permitted to roam our yard without supervision, I'd sneak through the neighbors' open back door and phone my parents from their kitchen. Once, the couple next door caught me in their house, but they thought I was after candy or cookies, and they actually invited me to stay for supper. I cleverly phoned my mother to let her know where I was—and then phoned again in the guise of the crank. For a seven-year-old, I had impeccable criminal instincts.

Why did I do it? Attention? Control? I honestly haven't a clue. I do remember the intense fear I felt when the police first visited our home, but also the wonder I experienced when I dialed my parents' number while those same officers conferred in our kitchen—and the genuine albeit inexplicable pleasure of hoodwinking them. One cop even put his hand on my shoulder, as I recollect, and told me not to be frightened of the phone calls. In another particularly audacious maneuver, I snuck into my grandmother's room while she was sleeping and phoned from under her bed. She was a fiercely loyal woman, my grandmother—and one with somewhat irreverent ideas regarding child-rearing. On a different occasion, when she caught me removing the insides of the ballpoint pens at the local branch bank, one of my unfortunate childhood hobbies, she didn't tell my parents. So it's very possible my grandmother did know what I was up to, or at least had her inklings—but if she did, she took the secret to the grave. As far as I'm aware, I am the only living person who knows the origin of those calls.

And then it ended. My father sat me down on the sofa in the living room ("Keep your feet off the sofa, please—that's the sofa your mother and I will die with.") and helped me memorize our new phone number. It was essential that I know each digit, in case an emergency should arise. Of course, after my parents paid for a new phone number, I wasn't fool enough to keep calling. Even at the age of seven, I knew which way madness lay. So life went on as it had before, as it does after earthquakes and typhoons, as it does after divorces and deaths and confessions. For a few months, a haunting silence hung over the house. Eventually we could no longer hear it.

. . . . Or maybe I still hear it just a little.

I confess that I wasn't fully truthful when I suggested that this episode has had no impact on who I am today. Rather— like a healed bone that aches to predict an unseen storm—the memory of my crimes surprises me when I least expect it. I will watch the media unmasking "Deep Throat" as W. Mark Felt and I will think: *I am next.* Or I'll hear about the Miami radio DJs fined 4,000 dollars for crank-calling Fidel Castro, pretending to be Venezuelan President Hugo Chavez, and I'll wonder if there's a statute of limitations on such offenses. (There is. I checked.) Even now, when I see a telephone company van parked in front of my parents' house, I'm always a bit apprehensive. It's not that I fear I'm going to be carted off in shackles—although you occasionally hear of people imprisoned decades after the fact for stealing poultry or absconding with library books. But I do fear exposure—because I don't want people rethinking me or my childhood. After all, I am no longer a seven-year-old maniac. I have now become the good kid everybody thought I was then.

My twinges of memory are strongest when I read about young children charged with serious offenses. It's ironic that the age of seven was the historical dividing line below which children could not be charged with crimes. (I can't help thinking: *"You must be taller than this line to ride this ride."*) When the media circus swirls around fifth graders accused of manslaughter or packs of preteen arsonists, I want to shout at the prosecutors not to give up on these kids. They might turn out just fine. Past performance is no indication of future unreliability. I have even impulsively considered calling the district attorneys in several egregious cases and telling my own story, but I'm not delusional enough to believe that they would listen. The odds are they'd hang up on me. Many adults still haven't learned the basic lessons regarding telephone etiquette and common decency that I figured out on my own somewhere between the ages of seven and eight.

When I finally sit down to confess to my parents, it is on the same sofa that my father once intended "to die with." The orange upholstery has faded to a deep shade of salmon, and the trim bears teeth marks from my sister-in-law's dog. One dark patch remains where bunny urine stained the damask—evidence that my mother has finally trained her rabbit to climb. The rest of the living room is in no better condition: rings from soda cans scar the end tables; the loveseat displays watermarks from a perennial leak in the roof. My father's new refrain is "One of these days we'll buy new furniture and then we'll start having guests over." But the state of the furniture is an excuse, not a reason. Except for family on holidays, he has not had guests over in fifteen years.

My parents themselves also show the signs of wear and tear. It is nice to think of them as middle-aged, but a cold assessment is that they're more than halfway done. My mother was once quite pretty; now she is good-looking *for her age.* My father, who always resembled a poor man's Groucho Marx, is starting to shrink. He may soon retire and spend all of his time battling the horseradish that has overrun his garden. It is twenty-three years since they fought a futile struggle with an unknown caller. Whatever they have gained in happiness, they have lost in joy.

I am not sure how to broach the subject. The episode seems so long ago, I almost think I've made it up entirely.

"Do you remember the crank caller?" I ask.

"Barely," says my father. "But your mother does. I bet she even remembers our old phone number."

My mother smiles and recites the number, on cue. I suspect she is thinking of my uncle—her brother-in-law—but she does not wish to stir up trouble.

"What made you think of that?" asks my father.

"I don't know how to say this. . . ."

"You know what we should have done," interjects my mother. "We should never have answered. We should have just let it ring and ring and ring. He would have tired himself out eventually."

She is probably correct. I hadn't thought of that before.

That's when I know I won't tell them. Ever. Because it will bring them no happiness or joy or even relief—just a bit of unnecessary consternation. They are much happier living with memories of the seven-year-old they think I was . . . and the right thing to do is to accept that. Confessions, after all, are fundamentally selfish. So instead of confessing, I sit beside my aging parents and think about that telephone ringing and ringing and ringing, its echo reverberating through the house. Someday I will call that same phone, I know, and nobody will be there to answer.

Two Cats, Fat and Thin

In fifth grade, we are asked to sacrifice: our prized possessions must be inventoried and surrendered to the state.

This is, mercifully, an exercise. I am a sheltered ten-year-old boy in an upscale bedroom suburb of New York City, a community so flush that its grade-school teachers must simulate hardship for their students. We have already suffered through a sugarless week in solidarity with the overtaxed colonists of eighteenth-century New England; we have wandered the classroom blindfolded, rendered sightless by a barrage of Confederate bullets. Now we are studying the immigrant experience—or possibly the Holocaust—and each of us has been ordered to bring from home a personal treasure that our teacher-turned-jailor, Mr. G., intends to "confiscate" as the price for our freedom. This crash course in palm-greasing takes place several years before the fall of the Berlin Wall, before the *Challenger* explosion, before the death of my beloved grandmother—and I confess the details are misty in my memory. (It is also an age of laxer classroom mores, when Mr. G. can still have his young charges massage his shoulders, not because he harbors ulterior designs on children, but because he enjoys having his muscles loosened.) What I do recall vividly is Mr. G. as Kafkaesque bureaucrat, shuffling between our tiny desks on his reconstructed knees, inspecting one boy's meticulously labeled coin collection and another girl's sepia photograph of her great-grandparents in fin de siècle Vienna. When he leans down to demand my offering, I gaze intensely into the Formica desktop. I have brought him nothing. I have not even told my parents that he'd asked.

"I don't have any favorite things," I mutter. "I'm sorry."

"Well, well," says Mr. G. "Nothing will come of nothing."

How can I know he's quoting *Lear?* I want to sink my teeth into his fleshy hand.

"Surely you must have *something* worth sacrificing," says Mr. G., sporting the perpetually bemused smile that defines his benevolent, leonine face. "Maybe you could bring in something for us later this week."

"All of my prized possessions have been taken!" I snap. "You're too late."

This earns me yet another afternoon with the school's psychologist.

Looking back now, I recall the prized possessions that I no longer possessed were two miniature rubber cats, one fat, one thin, given to me by my grandmother's eldest sister. The thin cat appeared hungry and scheming—a synthetic, feline Cassius. The fat cat looked as though he'd just swallowed an obese goldfish. They were not a matching pair, manufactured as companions, but two independent creatures forced into unsought friendship. Neither of them had real names. Merely Fat Cat and Thin Cat. Although they'd once been the most treasured objects of my brief existence—at the age of six, I had carried them everywhere, even into the bathtub—they lack any other social or economic value. Unfortunately, our school's psychologist, a tense, hyperanalytic fussbudget, got hung up on determining whether Aunt Emma was an aunt or a grandaunt. We never came around to discussing Fat and Thin, so my unspoken anxiety continued to slosh around inside me like battery acid. Even now, I shiver when I recall my private apocalypse.

It was the final autumn of the Carter presidency. My family was driving through northern Florida, en route to New York, because, to my mother, every commercial jet was an airborne coffin. She'd been arguing with my father, insisting that a presidential vote for John Anderson would throw the 1980 election to Reagan and usher in nuclear winter. We'd just visited my grandaunt in Miami Beach, the last time we would ever see her. I had my two travel companions, Fat and Thin, securely buckled into the backseat of my mother's foul-tempered Dodge Dart. I suppose my brother was also in the vehicle—he must have been about two years old—but I cannot be certain. I was too busy making sure that Fat and Thin didn't grow carsick and, later, that they were tucked under the covers in the gloomy motel room outside St. Augustine, where we'd all spend the night. We'd only entered the room long enough to inspect it—we hadn't even emptied our luggage from the trunk—but my cats decided to enjoy a nap, a fleeting, indolent snooze while the rest of the family ducked out for breakfast at the local Waffle House or Denny's. Who was I to insist otherwise? Maybe we also collected seashells and pink coral on the public beach. Or we scaled the ramparts of the historic Spanish fort. I have no reason to remember that breakfast, any more than I recall the events of the day, two months later, on which my father drew me aside, following dinner, to reveal that my grandaunt had succumbed to stomach cancer. No, that morning in St. Augustine was one without omens, all prologue to an unforeseen horror. How could I anticipate that, when we returned, joyful and sun-drunk, to our otherwise undisturbed motel room, both Fat and Thin would be gone?

As in any self-respecting whodunit, suspicion immediately fell upon the servants—in this case, any of the depleted, middle-aged African American maids who vacuumed and scrubbed toilets while the Caucasian guests scaled the Spanish battlements and collected pink coral on the beaches. These women had opportunity. They had motive. Who else would pilfer a pair of worthless rubber cats except a mother or grandmother too impoverished to purchase feline companions for her own brood? That's how my father explained it to me. I had lots of toys. Most likely the poor black child who'd been given Fat and Thin had none. Nor did my parents believe there was malice involved in the catnapping. Rather, entering an empty motel room that contained only two rubber cats, the well-intentioned maid probably believed the creatures had been abandoned. My parents pledged they would buy me new cats. *Better* cats. But to hope that Fat and Thin might return home was simply unrealistic. If we pursued the matter doggedly, a blameless working mother might lose her job. What good would that accomplish? Besides, even if it were possible, did I really want to yank these cheap, well-worn toys from the hands of a deprived little boy?

So we continued our journey up the seaboard. Past unmarked police cars scanning for Yankee plates, through palmetto thickets blanketed with Spanish moss. We drove by the hospital where, the previous winter, my mother had undergone emergency surgery after dropping a can of tomato soup on her left big toe. Soon the air turned crisp, and we crossed the endless brooks and runs of Virginia. Then Delaware, where I was bundled into a windbreaker and rewarded with a sour gumball. And New Jersey, an endless colonnade of chemical drums that looked like giant toadstools. Finally, we were back in New York, passing the playing fields where I would soon master the arts of lollygagging and wearing a baseball mitt on my head. We parked opposite the neighbor's stone wall—the wall that my brother would later reshape with the bumper of his first car.

But there were now only four of us in the vehicle, not six.

I stared out the windshield at our overlit house, the carefully timed lamps blazing in the upstairs windows, thinking of that needy boy back in Florida whose toilet-scrubbing mother couldn't afford to take vacations.

Did I really want to yank Fat and Thin from his deprived little hands?

Yes, I did. Yes, I did! YES, I DID!

Twenty years after the crime of *my* century—for Fat and Thin are my Great Train Robbery and Lindbergh baby and Manson family murders all rolled into one—I was hired to teach an introductory course in applied ethics at Brown University. Whether by coincidence or subconscious design, much of my syllabus focused on the countless moral questions surrounding property rights. Should my neighbor have to compensate me if she builds a house that obstructs my view? Why shouldn't private business owners be permitted to discriminate on the basis of race or religion? Who has the most convincing claim to a stolen painting that is subsequently sold and purchased in good faith by an unsuspecting third party? These are the conundrums that try eighteen-year-olds' souls, during those ephemeral salad days before they start amassing property of their own. When you ask them is it ethical for a poor maid to steal two cheap toys for her son from the motel room of a wealthy family, they grapple with the matter quite intensely. On the whole, they tend to be surprisingly forgiving of the well-intentioned and indigent cat burglar. Some even defend the working-class bandit who actually knows that the well-heeled family will return for the toys, yet steals them anyway, comparing the theft to pilfering apples for starving children or swallowing a phone company error in your favor. In contrast, my thirty-something friends—professional, civic-minded couples raising overindulged children of their own—see no ambiguity in the situation. Stealing is stealing. To the last they are surprisingly lacking in sympathy for the imaginary servant who, in my concocted scenario, makes off with a pair of hypothetical rubber cats.

Why are my Brown students so lenient? I often suspect it is because they have never before considered the injustice of a social system that allows some children to amass toys while others have none. Sure, they are aware of poverty: kwashiorkor and marasmus in the starving, dust-clad villages of the Sahel; hemorrhagic fevers ravaging war-torn swaths of the Congo. The more socially conscious among them feel guilty that they have the leisure to study Gramsci and feminist theory, while millions of their chronological peers work fast-food counters in urban ghettos and raise toddlers on public assistance. My students find these inequities fundamentally unsettling, even unjust—though, in all fairness, few will devote their lives to eradicating poverty and even fewer, if any, would voluntarily exchange places with their less fortunate brothers and sisters. What my students have never done, however, is reflect upon a life without toys. In a society where mass-produced plastic action figures cost ten dollars a piece and every middle-class family has a closet well-stocked with such wholesome board games as Monopoly and Risk, my students find "toylessness" as alien as homelessness. They side with the maid because, accustomed to an arsenal of Xboxes and multiethnic Barbie dolls whose shoe collections rival that of Imelda Marcos, they do not see much cost in losing two inexpensive toys. When I describe to them the vanished immigrant world in which my grandmother and Aunt Emma grew up, where one home-fashioned rag doll was handed down like a cache of jewels from sister to sister, they listen with tolerant incredulity. I might as easily be telling them that when I was their age, I hiked fifty miles to school every morning—uphill, both ways—through drifts of year-round snow.

Occasionally, of course, a student will take the side of the wealthy family. I recall one particular girl—a sharp-thinking beauty, well on her way toward professional school and civic-minded childrearing—who had already learned not to tinker with the rules of social organization. "What about the boy whose toys were stolen?" she wanted to know. "What if those were his most beloved possessions? What if they'd been given to him by his grandparents on their deathbeds?" I admired her eloquence, but I also sensed her passion was not personal— that she had never actually lost anything of value. "Think about what being victimized like that could do to somebody, particularly a small child," she urged her skeptical classmates. "For all you know, that kid will never get over his missing cats. For all you know, taking those cats away ruined his entire life."

I won't claim that the loss of Fat and Thin ruined my life, but their disappearance certainly changed it. Even today, I am a far more cautious—even suspicious—person than I might have been if not for that episode. I am particularly careful not to leave shopping bags in my car while I run a few additional errands or an attaché case at a restaurant table when I visit the restroom. I never loan out my door keys, not even to a close friend or relative for a matter of seconds. When I travel, I phone my home answering machine at least once a day—not principally to check my messages, but to assure myself that my apartment building hasn't burned down. (I still have an answering machine, probably among the last few on Manhattan's Upper West Side.) And every morning, if I'm staying at a hotel, I pack up all of my belongings and stash them inside the trunk of my car. So while I give generously to charity and even to panhandlers, no slippery-fingered room cleaner's toddler will ever acquire a stray sock or a ballpoint pen at my expense. Of course, even without the St. Augustine massacre, I might have grown into a thoroughly maladjusted adult. Hitler and Stalin could still have proven butchers, notwithstanding loving childhoods. What I can say with confidence is that not a day passes during which I don't actively fear being robbed of what I care about most deeply: not tangible objects, but friendships and loved ones. I imagine psychiatry has a label for this walking dread. That is why I don't see a psychiatrist.

Another consequence of this traumatic incident has been my longstanding discomfort with the housekeeping staff at hotels and motor lodges. The winter after Fat and Thin disappeared, I slammed the door in the face of another African American motel maid—this time on the resort island of Sanibel—and nearly shattered her nose. The woman, a plump battle-axe with a solitary gold tooth, accused me of racism. My prejudice, of course, was of a different sort. Alas, my parents, who had long since moved beyond the previous autumn's horrors, forced me to apologize. Later that week, my father drove our rental car through the shanty towns where the cleaning staff lived, so that I might witness the corrugated zinc roofs and the undergarments drying in the open air. Yet what most interested me were the dozens of young children scampering among the chickens and guinea fowl. I scrutinized them carefully, wondering if one of these boys might somehow have acquired Fat or Thin from a cousin who lived farther upstate. I had long ago given up hope of recovering *both* of my cats. My deal with the cosmos was that if *one* of them returned home, I would behave irreproachably forever. Many nights I lay awake in bed, trying to determine whether I would prefer the jovial, fun-loving Fat or the wise, worldly Thin. I was trapped forever in my own microversion of *Sophie's Choice*. Whatever the outcome of my fantasies, I ended up sobbing myself to sleep.

I am self-aware enough to recognize that while stealing may be stealing, the loss of the rubber cats was far more than merely the loss of the rubber cats. My aunt had died, after all—or my grandaunt, to please the sticklers. Even at the age of six, I understood that this was the ultimate of all calamities, a disaster so unspeakably horrific that we pretend the suffering is bearable and struggle on with our lives. Many people close to me have died since that evening when my father explained that we wouldn't be visiting Miami Beach anymore, but I'll never shake the genuine terror I felt when he revealed the true course of human events. I'd been introduced to the ghastly secret that separated the adults from the children: members of the species *Homo sapiens* were like rubber cats. You could return to your motel room one night to find them gone forever.

My aunt was one of six siblings, all deceased, only two of whom produced biological children. One brother, Harry, eloped with a non-Jewish woman and was banished from the life of the family forever. A second brother, Morris, traveled by train to California at the end of World War II—and his children, in perpetual exile, are prosperous restaurateurs in Los Angeles. While I think of Emma's sister, Ida, as my grandmother, she is technically my mother's stepmother. (My biological grandmother discovered a lump in her breast in 1953 and was sent home from the hospital to die.) The comedian Jerry Lewis is a distant cousin, as was the stage actor Bert Lahr, but neither Lewis nor Lahr's son, John, have answered my multiple letters. Little close family remains to pay respects at Aunt Emma's gravesite at Mount Ararat, in Queens, where she is buried alongside her parents and thousands of unfortunate strangers. When I visit, on a warm autumn afternoon nearly twenty-five years after her death, the markers are over-run with desiccated vines and thorny creepers.

It is amazing how little I know of my aunt. She was born in 1898 and worked her entire adult life as an executive secretary at the Allied Chemical and Dye Corporation. She never married. As far as my surviving cousins recall, she never dated. Most of her time was spent in the company of another single woman, Alice McCarthy, but whether they were merely friends or romantically involved is a mystery lost to the ages. What I do remember are visits to her single-occupancy apartment in the old Sherry Netherland Hotel, and how she showed me a paperweight made from glass-encased butterfly wings. And I remember vividly the evening she gave me Fat Cat and Thin Cat, after a quiet afternoon during which I downed numerous glasses of chocolate milk and she nibbled fruit-flavored baby food, the only meal her esophageal strictures permitted. That is *all* I remember of my grandmother's eldest sister. Yet I still love this octogenarian spinster, who is now but a smattering of flashbulb memories in my consciousness, comprising an image of a perpetually impish woman with dimpled cheeks and a penchant for turquoise hats. I remember loving her, and I remember her loving me. I still own the butterfly paperweight, one of the few possessions I carry with me from apartment to apartment. Alongside this heirloom, there is always an empty space on the shelf, a final resting place perpetually waiting for Fat or Thin. I am like a war mother, keeping free a chair for her missing son. At some point reason eclipses hope, but the opening must remain as a tribute to the long departed.

Two months after I visited my aunt's gravesite, I found myself once again on the east coast of Florida for the wedding of a childhood friend. I made the terrible mistake of staying in the Best Western at 1505 Belvedere Road in West Palm Beach—an error I wish to encourage all readers of this essay to avoid. The motel appeared a suitable enough lodging at first glance—not too pricey—although the soda machines didn't work and assorted household debris floated atop the pool. Lulled into lowering my guard by the lush, subtropical air and the swaying palms, I took the risk of packing only my computer into my trunk and leaving my other belongings inside the motel room while I attended the nuptials, wearing a tuxedo. How could I ever have anticipated that the housekeeping staff would confuse the day of my departure? When I returned at two A.M., feeling festive but fatigued to the bone, I discovered that the maid had turned over the room in my absence. She'd carried with her my beach clothes, my toiletries, even the prescription medication that I take before traveling on airborne coffins. To this day, despite my repeated pleas, the motel has proven unable to track down my missing belongings. I will not keep an open space on my shelf for them.

Of course, as a result of this screwup, I found myself with a day to kill on the Florida coast, lacking so much as a bathing suit to wear or a paperback novel to read. Seized with an irrational impulse, I immediately phoned my mother in New York and asked her for the name of the motel where the rubber cats had disappeared. "Which rubber cats?" she asked. When she finally understood what I wanted to know, it became clear that she possessed only the faintest memory of the entire episode. My father didn't remember the rubber cats at all. That left me no choice but to drive up the seaboard toward St. Augustine—intent on stopping at each roadside motel. I didn't care about my recently appropriated toothbrush. I was thinking of my long-lost friends.

My plan was to scour the city, making inquiries of desk clerks. Yet what could I possibly ask? Do you recall if I left a pair of rubber cats here thirty-two years ago? Would you mind if I asked your housekeeping staff if they'd stolen my toys? As I drove past the Pelican Island Wildlife Refuge and the Kennedy Space Center, the absurdity of my scheme grew increasingly clear to me. The woman who had made off with my prized possessions would be long-since retired. Or worse. Her son might well have a six-year-old boy of his own. Most likely, the motel itself had been purchased by a national chain and then sold off again in a series of complex transactions that might well have concluded with a wrecking ball. The bottom line was that any sane motel clerk would have laughed me out of his lobby before I made it within shouting distance of a housekeeper. I would have had as much luck convincing Dellwood Foods to put the cats' photographs on its milk cartons. So I turned my car around and drove back—to my bare motel room, to the life I lead without my childhood toys.

The irony, I realize, is that if I could find the grown man who'd been that deprived child, I would let him keep the cats. Gladly. I can't say I would have at the age of fifteen or even at twenty-five—but as a thirty-four-year-old university professor, I've finally found enough peace in life to forgive the misguided motel maid who did me a small injustice a quarter of a century ago. Honestly, I don't even want to see the cats again. Fat and Thin are far more vivid in my memory than they could ever be on a stranger's shelf—or even, for all I know, on his pillow. So what do I want from this man whom I will never meet—this man who probably doesn't even know that I exist—this man who has never even once asked himself where his mother or grandmother found the toys she brought home from work? All I want is to see who he is—to discover what became of the boy whose mother gave him a pair of rubber cats, one fat, one thin, on a fateful autumn night in 1980. That's what I want to ask him: did they change his life as much as they changed mine?

Mr. Odd and Mr. Even

My maternal grandfather, Jacob Henry Friedman, answered to "Jimmy" on the streets of New York's Lower East Side, but at Tulane Medical School he assumed the alias Jack Murphy. The story, as it currently survives, goes something like this: On his first day in Louisiana, my mother's father was invited to the university by a hand-delivered note for a tête-à-tête with the dean of students. I can picture Grandpa Jimmy, the son of a Carpathian cigar roller, hurriedly donning his store-bought suit—most likely the smallest size available at Orhbach's or Klein's—and crossing the drowsy, elm-lined campus at the fastest clip his stunted legs could muster. What were his thoughts? I'll venture he feared that the admissions committee had made an error, much as I similarly feared, eight decades later, when I received my own letter of acceptance to medical school—and that he'd been summoned in order to rectify the mistake. Yet for my grandfather, in 1924, the stakes were far higher: he had already relocated his entire family to New Orleans, where he shared a two-room student apartment with his middle-aged parents and his demented grandmother. The living arrangement sounds like a scene from a Woody Allen film, but for my relatives it was a cost-cutting measure of considerable gravity. So maybe Grandpa Jimmy feared that the dean had learned of this unorthodox living arrangement and wanted the Austrian Family Friedman dispatched back to Delancey Street posthaste.

A painting of the Tulane campus from this period hangs in my father's study: undergraduates in jackets and ties strolling beneath blankets of dense Spanish moss. How elegant and genteel these young men look! And how brimming with vigor! They were, after all, the future governors and oil barons of the Gulf Coast—that last generation of tarnished statesmen who would fight to defend segregation. The Kingfish himself, Huey Long, had dropped out of the law school only a few years before. All of which may explain why the dean of medicine, remembered in my family as a benevolent old patrician, believed my fast-talking, leaden-legged Jewish-socialist-atheist granddad might benefit from a pep talk and a name change. I can imagine the white-suited dean slapping Grandpa Jimmy on the back, maybe provoking a wheeze, and offering him a hand-rolled cigar or a glass of imported cognac, although I can't prove any of this actually transpired. All I know is that the dean advised my grandfather he would find little if any anti-Semitism in Louisiana, and certainly none at the university—yet, just the same, doors might open more easily for a student called Jack Murphy than one named Jacob Friedman. *Why make it any harder on yourself? What's so wrong with putting your best foot forward?* So my grandfather, who desired to become a surgeon more than he despised smug apologists, swallowed a pound of fleshy pride, and introduced himself around the physiology laboratory the next morning by his adopted name. Later, after he'd returned to New York and given up surgery for psychiatry, my grandfather would call "Jack Murphy" his *southern name.* Ironically he'd also insist that he'd encountered far less anti-Semitism in Louisiana than up north, which may indeed have been true. After all, in Dixie he was Murphy, not Friedman. How all of this name changing affected my great-grandparents Sadie and Willie isn't entirely clear, but the immigrant couple retained their own "northern" names through the whole four years of their son's medical education.

Meanwhile, in the Yiddish-speaking ghetto of Antwerp, Belgium, my father's father attended drafting and metallurgy classes as *Shmuel Aryeh,* which translates into "Sammy the Lion"—a name fit for a Chasidic mobster. The church-operated trade school catered primarily to working-class boys, nearly all Catholics, but admitted a handful of talented Jewish youths from the bustling refugee community around the central rail station. None of my grandfather's instructors ever suggested that he change his name. What good would that have done a thirteen-year-old kid sporting a skullcap and unshorn sideburns? However, the straight-laced nuns who taught the school's mandatory courses in French composition and Dutch literature provided their Semitic charges with additional monikers, including "*sale Juif*" (dirty Jew) and "*Christusmoordenaar*" (Christ killer) often punctuated with the slap of a yardstick across the boys' bare palms. Late in life, as his mind softened in suburban New York, my grandfather would accost nuns in McDonald's and harangue them in Flemish. But at the time, with Léon Degrelle's pro-Nazi Parti Rexiste holding mass rallies of dockworkers at the port, my grandfather swallowed the slurs and smacks of Belgian bigotry without retaliation. When Catholic churchgoers pelted Grandpa's family with rocks on the stroll home from their Sunday services or Easter masses—the Flemish children shouting, "Go back to Palestine," a land my grandfather had never seen—Shmuel Aryeh didn't gather the stones and return fire, as did some of his classmates. Instead he ducked under a pushcart with his sisters and hid. I suspect it was during one of these attacks, or a similar episode, that he first consciously formed an understanding of his life's guiding principle: "Never, ever, stick your neck out." That's probably good advice when you're hiding from a mob of middle-class churchgoers lobbing stones, but my grandfather applied it universally.

Whether it was foresight or panic that drove my grandfather out of Europe isn't all too clear, but by the time Field Marshal Fedor von Bock's panzers swept across the Low Countries, the Belgian branch of the Appel family was safely ensconced in the Bronx. (The Romanian branch of the family died en masse at Auschwitz-Birkenau, as best we can guess, along with my grandfather's school chums who'd fought back against the stone throwers.) When he was inside his mother's Fox Street apartment, my grandfather wore his skullcap and spoke only in Yiddish, and he followed rigidly the Hebraic dietary laws. Yet in the jewelry district on Manhattan's 6th Avenue, where he set gems for wealthy gentiles, he performed his work bareheaded and ate non-Kosher cold cuts served up by a colleague's spouse. For Saturday—the Sabbath—he assured his parents that he was attending services at a synagogue across town; instead he returned to his shop and appraised the rubies and emeralds that had piled up, like children's beads, during the week. My grandfather led two parallel lives, one moderately religious and the other moderately secular, but both motivated by his desire to keep the ship of life from shaking. When the Democrats asked him to campaign door-to-door for a local judge, he did so gladly—not because he shared the man's politics, or even understood them, but because the majority of his acquaintances were Democrats. He became a fan of Tom Mix Westerns because Tom Mix was all the rage at the moment. He sported bow ties because he thought them less assuming. The only time my grandfather ever bucked the establishment was when he challenged a two-dollar parking ticket that he'd received for leaving his Plymouth on a grassy median after being specifically instructed to do so by a crossing guard at a public beach. He won his case—evidence that the system worked—and, fifty years later, he was still recounting this fleeting moment of courtroom drama. I can picture my grandfather as a paunchy, mustached young man in his one good suit—hand-tailored by his American-born bride to fit his four foot, eleven inch, frame—vowing to tell the truth before an indifferent traffic magistrate. "I, Leo Sander Appel, do solemnly swear. . . ." *Leo Sander.* All that remained of Sammy the Lion. Because my grandfather had as much of the Yiddish mobster in him as Anne Frank. In fact, his experience with the parking ticket flummoxed him so greatly that shortly afterward he gave the Plymouth's keys to my grandmother, and he never drove a motor vehicle again.

While American GIs fought to reclaim Antwerp from Hitler's minions and Luftwaffe shells leveled the stone row house on the Terlisstraat, where my father's father had so recently studied Talmud, Grandpa Jimmy—now a headshrinker—ran a military facility for the criminally insane in Santa Fe, New Mexico. These were men who'd shot their commanding officers, eighteen-year-old kids who'd cracked up after months of atoll-hopping in the Pacific. But I suspect there were also a good number of run-of-the-mill deserters and homosexual men, as well as others who failed to meet the spit-and-polish demands of infantry life. If Herman Wouk's Captain Queeg had served in the army, rather than the navy, he would likely have ended up supine on Colonel Friedman's couch. What is remarkable to me is how many of these men my grandfather genuinely befriended. This was an era when the boundaries between psychiatrist and patient remained far more fluid than they are today: even ten years later, my mother was still clearing the place settings from the family's dining room, which doubled as Grandpa Jimmy's home office, so that he could perform electroshock therapy on the oak-and-mahogany tabletop. So it must have seemed perfectly natural for Colonel Friedman—Grandpa Leo reverently called him "the full colonel"—to accompany his patients to baseball games and to invite them over for suppers with his stunning young wife and darling infant daughter. Once he accompanied a black patient to Chicago and, decked out in his stylish dress uniform with gold epaulets and sundry medals, walked the man through the front door of the "whites only" dining room at the Palmer House. They were seated in a distant corner of the restaurant, but they were served—nobody wanting to deny a "full colonel" at the height of the war, even if he'd brought along a "Negro" guest. In short Grandpa Jimmy made a point of sticking his neck out as far as his tiny, rounded shoulders would permit.

These were not easy years for the Family Friedman. The infant daughter—so beloved, so fragile—died unexpectedly and was buried the following morning in the high country of New Mexico, her very memory concealed like the evidence of a pernicious crime. I was in my thirties before I learned of her existence. Then the mother, Sadie, collapsed from Stokes-Adams disease, a rare heart condition that was 100 percent fatal then, although today it is thoroughly benign. But the coup de grâce was when the young wife, the first Ida, found a lump on her breast and then died when her second daughter, my mother, had just turned eight years old. Dr. Friedman told neither the patient nor her daughter that she was dying. Yet these tragedies only tested my maternal grandfather; they did not temper him. After the war he set up a psychiatry practice on the Grand Concourse that specialized in bending rules for the sake of "the public welfare": certifying elective abortions as medically necessary to circumvent New York State's pre–*Roe vs. Wade* statute; offering pro bono testimony for indigent offenders pleading insanity. In his spare time, Grandpa Jimmy took his motherless daughter to Negro League baseball games, where they were the only Caucasian spectators, and, when she turned nine, he sent her to buy bait alone from his preferred tackle shop in the roughest section of East Harlem.

Everybody who speaks of my grandfather during this period describes him as *extremely* likeable and crazy. Or sometimes: likeable and *extremely* crazy. He was the sort of man who one expected to demand that voting be halted—and the election commissioner summoned—so that he could write in the name of a left-wing candidate during the presidential primary. "Nobody has ever asked us for a write-in ballot before," the local supervisor in this uniformly Democratic district had explained. "We don't know how to do that." Grandpa Jimmy had listened to the man patiently, as he might a full-blown psychotic, and then he'd answered decisively: "Well, you'll learn." And, like Grandpa Leo, Grandpa Jimmy also had his personal run-in with law enforcement. While driving through rural Virginia, returning to New York City after his army service in New Mexico, he was stopped by the state police for speeding, for failing to obey numerous traffic signals, and for driving without a valid license or registration. The state trooper ordered him to wait in his car while the officer returned to his own cruiser to copy down the identifying information from Grandpa Jimmy's military ID. However, as soon as the cop entered his own vehicle, my grandfather hit the accelerator . . . and, fifteen minutes later, he was on the Chesapeake auto ferry bound for Maryland, with Virginia's shoreline receding into the distance. I imagine there's still a warrant out for him. "I would have paid the ticket," he later told his second wife. "But I wasn't about to miss my ferry."

Grandpa Leo also did his part for the war effort, but as a buck private serving in Anniston, Alabama. He'd combed the South Bronx to find a military doctor willing to certify that he was five feet tall, so he'd be eligible for enlistment—far better than to stand out at the sidelines. (He did not find Grandpa Jimmy, but a surgeon named Charles Halberstam—the father of historian David Halberstam—was more than happy to slide a phonebook under Grandpa Leo's feet.) Why the army chose to station a Belgian metalworker fluent in six European languages at a training camp in the Appalachian foothills for the duration of the war is one of those mysteries only Joseph Heller could unravel—but as his bunkmates shipped out to North Africa and Normandy, my grandfather sorted documents and delivered packages at Fort McClellan. He eventually got himself attached to the Sixty-ninth Infantry Division—not the famed "Fighting 69th" Infantry *Regiment*—but a division later known around Anniston for an episode in which my grandfather, along with thirty other New York servicemen, overturned a public bus when the white driver refused a seat to a pregnant black woman. It was permissible to stick one's neck out, I suppose, when surrounded by other necks. It was also less dangerous, I imagine, if you were soon departing the continent. Yet, true to form, when my grandmother shared this story with the family sixty years later, my grandfather pleaded with me not to write about it—fearful that the military authorities might still come after him.

Alas the military authorities appear to have been generally indifferent to my grandfather, if they were even cognizant of his existence. When the day arrived for the Sixty-ninth Division to ship out to reinforce General Clark in the Apennines, the name Leo Sander Appel was mysteriously dropped from the embarkation list. So, instead of liberating the Italians from Mussolini, Grandpa Leo returned home to New York City on leave and proposed to my grandmother, whom he'd met on a total of three previous occasions, but who hailed from a good, quiet family that didn't stick its neck out. His bride's parents kept a clean home. They were neither too secular nor too religious. Goldilocks, if she'd sought a Jewish household, would have found the accommodations to her liking. Moreover, the favorite expression of my grandmother's Lithuanian-born father was, "Don'ts be rocking the boat"—which suited Grandpa Leo's understanding of both grammar and life. He also liked that his future father-in-law worked as a professional candler, examining eggs for embryonic chickens, a task that required both steady hands and infinite patience.

The Eisenhower years matched my grandfather's temperament, and he did his utmost to keep his family contented and inconspicuous. When his acquaintances moved from the city to the suburbs, he followed, settling into a garden apartment where the neighbors raised potted geraniums and draped flags from their windows on Independence Day. He invited these neighbors over for tea and cards, whether he liked them or not. *Liking* them wasn't the point. *Getting along* with them was what mattered. As did so many refugees of his generation, he refused to teach his children French or Dutch or Yiddish. He told them nothing of the stone-throwing churchgoers, never mentioned the boyhood friends who'd been deported to the camps. The man's goal was to raise a respectable, unobtrusive brood who could "earn their own bread" and "not step on anybody's toes." To this end my grandfather brought home three polished silver dollars from his jewelry shop every Friday afternoon, one for each of his three children. They were not to spend these, of course. These coins were treasures to be saved for their educations—their futures—so that they'd never know the plight of a penniless refugee. Alas my grandfather's entrepreneurial skills did not keep pace with even these modest ambitions. By the age of forty, he was bankrupt and saddled with three young mouths to feed. My grandmother reclaimed the silver dollars and shelled them out, one by one, to purchase groceries for the family.

Eventually Grandpa Leo found employment at another man's jewelry shop, earning slave wages for his skilled labor. He walked five miles to work each morning because my grandmother had children to look after and he refused to drive a car. But on those long walks he developed a corollary to his theory of the universe—one that incorporated economics into his existing theology of unobtrusiveness. Grandpa Leo faced the following dilemma: how could one guarantee oneself financial security without taking any risks? Certainly not by operating one's own business, he'd discovered. But then his thoughts drifted to the successful men he'd known—maybe even to Dr. Charles Halberstam sliding that phonebook under his shoes—and he concluded that the field of medicine offered the solution to all of life's challenges. It was too late for him, obviously. But he decided, on the spot, that both of his sons were to become physicians. They had no choice in the matter. To do otherwise would be to fail life's greatest test. Life's *only* test. Even after his mind went soft, in the nursing home, the man would take the hands of the young doctors and nurses and urge them to go to medical school.

My two grandfathers finally met on Thanksgiving Day, 1969. In the course of western civilization, their encounter doesn't rank with Stanley embracing Livingstone or with Proust and Joyce's cab ride home from Stravinsky's *Le Renard*—although in their own lives the rendezvous was certainly as momentous. Grandpa Jimmy only had one daughter. Although Grandpa Leo had three children, my father—a second-year medical student—was by far the most marriageable. So Grandpa Leo and Grandma Lillian were thrilled to drive to the Bronx for a dinner served on the oak and mahogany tabletop where my mother's father had once shocked depressives, and Grandpa Jimmy and my mother's stepmother, the second Ida, were more than pleased to host them. Yet beyond these rudimentary recollections, clouded by time and hindsight, the details of the evening remain quite dim. The most my living grandmother can recall is that it snowed a lot and she had difficulty finding a parking space.

Did Grandpa Jimmy advocate atheism over the sideboard? Did he explain to his guests why he'd supported Eugene McCarthy in the previous presidential election? Probably not. Most likely he sat peacefully through Grandpa Leo's short Hebrew prayer and then praised the *tsimmes* and pineapple-lacquered yams that Leo's wife had prepared for the visit. However, I don't imagine it wouldn't have mattered if Grandpa Jimmy had indeed dished out a disquisition on Freud and Marx and the political philosophy of Malcolm X. Grandpa Leo was just happy that his son was marrying a physician's daughter— psychiatrists *were* M.D.s after all, better than dentists—and how could anyone doubt a man who'd risen to the rank of full colonel?

The best I can estimate is that they stuck close to the same holiday script that our family would adhere to for many years to come: the same recipes, the same conversations, the same concerns about "saving room for dessert" and what might happen to the leftovers. And, at the conclusion of the evening's festivities, wine glass in his elevated hand, I'm sure my grandfather offered the young couple a variant of his perennial toast.

"They should live to be one hundred twenty," declared Grandpa Leo.

"So should we all," responded Grandpa Jimmy.

They'd become a team now, these two mismatched men who, beyond children in love, shared nothing but height. The patriarchs emptied their glasses, and the other guests sipped politely, thinking for a brief moment of that distant future. I can picture Grandpa Leo and Grandpa Jimmy, at opposite ends of the table, united in hope.

One of these men, now approaching ninety, continues his march toward twelve decades. The other man was dead within three years.

It might so easily have been otherwise. Grandpa Leo might have been the one to mistake his angina pains for a stomach ulcer and to suffer a massive heart attack before the birth of his first grandchild. He'd certainly faced his share of scares over the decades: a burst appendix, a severe concussion against a flagstone step, an emergency cholecystectomy during an era when gallbladder extraction was still an open and challenging procedure. So it could have been Grandpa Jimmy who took me hunting for acorns in the park, brought me chocolate milkshakes on visiting day at summer camp, and welcomed my birthdays with envelopes full of five- and ten-dollar bills. But it wasn't. We often play "counter-history" on the grandest scale, like modern-day Tolstoys, asking what would have happened had Napoleon triumphed at Waterloo. And what if Roosevelt had succumbed to polio? Or if Sirhan's bullets had targeted Nixon and not RFK? It's painless to speculate about a world in which South defeats North, or Gore squeaks past Bush, far harder to reinvent your own life with a different cast of characters. Yet I am who I am because a man I never met dismissed a blocked artery as indigestion.

Soon my own medical training will be complete, and I will have to choose: do I pursue the secure life of a physician or the equally strenuous, but far more risky, profession of writing? I can hear Grandpa Leo warning me: *Who raised you to stick out your neck? And if you try to do both, you could end up doing neither.* He is dying now, his brain as soppy as a saturated sponge. Maybe I owe him this legacy, this one last concession. But, from a distance, I can also hear Grandpa Jimmy urging: *Watch out or they'll try to "Jack Murphy" you! If you make the rules, young man, eventually you win the game.* Both men speak with love. Each is confident that his path is the only true road to happiness. And I stand between them—wanting to please each, knowing that it will be impossible to satisfy either of them fully. Instead I carry them both with me, tugged now one way by the man who took part in nearly every event of my life, now the other way by a man who never experienced any of them. Maybe that is the greatest of wonders: that we can be shaped so much by those we've known closely, and equally by those we've never known at all—and that we too can change the world long after we've left it.

The Man Who Was Not
My Grandfather

In his early eighties, my grandfather—happily married for six decades and rendered impotent by prostate cancer—received a desperate letter from a woman he had dated while on military leave from the United States Army in 1943. All I knew of Blanche was that she'd once been trapped with Grandpa Leo for many hours atop an amusement park ride at Coney Island, that she'd been substantially overweight in her twenties, and that my grandparents exchanged cards with her and her husband every Jewish New Year. In short she wasn't even a supporting actress in our family's saga, but a mere extra, a woman who had strolled across the background of our past and vanished into the ether of time and memory. All that changed—at least momentarily—when her Rosh Hashanah missive arrived, penned in a caregiver's hand, announcing that the unfortunate lady was recently widowed, newly blind, and consigned to a nursing home in a distant outer borough of New York City. "Will you please come visit me?" she asked. Her invitation pointedly included Grandma Lillian as well.

My grandfather shared the contents of the letter with our family over our holiday dinner that weekend. He seemed surprised by the request and saddened at Blanche's condition, but nothing in his tone or manner revealed even the remotest inkling of affection for a woman whom he hadn't seen in sixty-one years. His greatest concern appeared to be the length of the bus trip to her facility.

"I suppose we *have* to visit her, now that she's asked," said Grandpa Leo—his voice utterly devoid of romance. He turned to my young cousin and added, "Visiting the sick is a true *mitzvah,* but never stay with them too long."

That prompted my aunt to recount—for my cousin's benefit—the comedic tale of my grandfather's sojourn with Blanche atop the amusement-park ride during a lightning storm. Then my father and my aunt each offered to drive my grandparents to the widow's nursing home. "We can even go next weekend," suggested my aunt. "Whatever works best for you."

My grandmother had remained silent during this conversation. She'd always been an extraordinarily easygoing person, I should emphasize, certainly not one prone to jealousy or spite. She'd also never met Blanche, as far as I knew, and she had no reason to dislike the blind widow other than that the woman had once dated my grandfather. So we were all dumb-founded to see my grandmother in tears.

"If you visit that woman, Leo," she warned between sobs, "I'm not going to let you back in our house. Am I making myself clear?"

Grandma Lillian could not have been clearer. Nor, when pressed by my father, was she willing to explain herself. "I'm his wife and she's not," said my grandmother. "That's the only explanation anyone needs." So neither of them visited Blanche, and they received no more New Year's cards. My grandparents' marriage continued happily for another four years, until my grandfather succumbed to his cancer, and during that time none of us ever again dared to raise the subject of Blanche's request.

My aunt—maybe because her own marriage had been such an unhappy one—has always taken an interest in our family's past. Her interest magnified after my grandfather's death, and it was through her efforts to chart my grandmother's geneal-ogy that I first learned of the man who was not my grand-father. That is the best way I have to describe the handsome young Latvian Jew my grandmother didn't marry—because even today I still do not know his name. My grandmother insists that she no longer remembers it, and although I do not believe her, I have stopped asking.

We were seated in my grandmother's kitchen, several months after my grandfather's funeral, and my aunt spread across the tabletop a pair of faded photographs that she had acquired from our cousins. One was a group portrait: here frowned the portly, double-chinned sisters of Grandma Lillian's father and their phalanx of stone-faced adult children, three rows of Litman cousins decked out for a long-forgotten wedding. In the foreground stood a brigade of sepia toddlers, boys and girls who would now have been in their late seventies. The other photograph depicted one of my grandmother's aunts and her offspring: five daughters endowed with zaftig peasant beauty, and a dashing, mustached son who might have passed for an Italian film star.

"He looks like Rudolf Valentino," I said, admiring my grandmother's cousin. "It's hard to believe that he's actually related to us." Nobody else in our short, round-faced family, to phrase matters delicately, displays similar Hollywood potential. "Are you sure he wasn't a changeling?"

"You never met him, Mom, did you?" asked my aunt.

"How could I meet him? He was in Europe and I was here." My grandmother dipped a donut into her coffee mug. "I was supposed to marry him, you know, but I wouldn't go through with it. Why should I marry a man I'd never met?"

"You were supposed to marry him?" my aunt asked incredulously.

"To get them out of Europe. Before the war," said Grandma Lillian. "The plan was for us to get married . . . and then his parents and all of his sisters would come over with him.

Maybe his nieces and nephews too. It was my father's idea." I could sense a strain of irritation rising in my grandmother's voice, as though the wedding proposal had just been pitched to her anew. "Who was *he* to tell *me* who to marry?"

"You couldn't have married your cousin *on paper*?" I asked. "And then divorced him as soon as he arrived in the United States?"

"Whoever thought of such craziness back then? It wasn't like things are now. If you got married, you got married and stayed married. Nobody got divorced."

"So what happened?" I asked.

"Nothing happened," she answered. "I married your grandfather."

"But what happened to your cousin and his family?"

My grandmother looked at me as though I'd asked her if the earth were flat. "I imagine they all died in the war," she said, matter-of-fact. "My father never mentioned them again. It wasn't something we talked about in those days."

"So we don't know for sure," I offered. "They *could* have survived. Maybe we can find them. . . ."

"They died in the war," Grandma said firmly. "Can't you leave it at that?"

"Do you remember their names?" I inquired—thinking that I might search for them or their children on the Internet. "Do you know what town they came from?"

"Why do you ask so many questions?" My grandmother sighed. "That's all I remember," she said. "Now let's talk about something else."

I would like to report that there is more to this story—that I tracked down the man who was not my grandfather, or his children, and discovered that my cousins had passed the war hiding out in a gentile's attic or had survived the selection at Auschwitz. The brutal reality is that all of the Litmans who remained in Latvia were likely shot by German Einsatzgruppen in late 1941 or starved to death in the Daugavpils Ghetto in early 1942. According to survivor-turned-historian Sidney Iwens, of the roughly 16,000 Jewish inhabitants of the region where my grandmother's family lived, fewer than one hundred escaped the Nazi death machine. So if there is any story still to be told, it is not of how my cousins survived the war, but of how my otherwise caring and gold-hearted grandmother allowed her father's family to be massacred. That is the Holocaust narrative we rarely tell, the opposite of Anne Frank and *Schindler's List,* the tale of those who did not make the sacrifices necessary to save the lives of others. Or maybe it is not a story at all, but the human condition, so unexceptional as not to be noteworthy. For there are many strangers whom *I* could likely save at this very moment—via sham marriage—from starvation or malaria or subjugation, only these women are not my cousins, and nobody has overtly asked me to marry them, so I give very little thought to my role in their plight. The bottom line is that heroism and altruism make better literary themes than self-interest. The histories of the man who does *not* visit his blind ex-girlfriend and of the woman who does *not* save the life of her cousin are tales that we do not like to hear.

My grandmother is now ninety years old. She lives alone in the same garden apartment where she raised her three children—two physicians and a teacher—watching black-and-white films and painting landscapes and churches copied from picture postcards. I visit her every week, knowing that each time I walk up her front stairs may be the last. I have no desire to cause her any stress or anxiety. But several months ago, I ventured one final salvo at learning more about her relationship with the man who was not my grandfather. My aunt had recently dropped in to display another set of family photos, so the moment seemed opportune.

"I've been meaning to ask you something," I ventured. "That cousin you were supposed to marry. Do you ever feel bad that you didn't marry him?"

A puzzled expression panned across my grandmother's face—and, at first, I feared she might not remember the cousin at all. But quickly, she found that isolated compartment in her memory.

"Why should I feel bad?" she demanded.

"Because if you'd married him," I said, "he wouldn't have died in the war."

I confined the death toll to one. I did not have the courage to mention his sisters.

"I suppose not," my grandmother agreed—as though this possibility has never before entered her mind. She gazed thoughtfully at her coffee mug. "But if I'd married him, I wouldn't have married your grandfather. *You* wouldn't exist."

That was true, of course, but my grandmother and her dashing cousin would have had other children, and my grandfather would have married someone else—possibly Blanche—and it is not clear that the world would have been any worse off, merely different. A generation of moral philosophers has grappled with how to place value on the lives of people who do not yet exist and how to compare their worth with the lives of those who already do exist, but such a conversation is well beyond my grandmother's inclinations or her twelfth-grade education. To her it's not even a tradeoff—that she let her cousin die, and thus my father and his siblings lived. The decision transcends cost-benefit analysis. It simply is what it is. She married my grandfather, not the man who was not my grandfather, and there is nothing more to discuss.

"Can I ask you one more thing?" I asked.

"You and your questions."

"Do you remember when Grandpa received that letter from his ex-girlfriend, Blanche, when she was in the hospital?" I asked. "Why didn't you want to visit her?"

"Why *should* I want to visit her?"

"I'm just surprised it mattered so much to you after sixty years."

"Sixty years is like yesterday. You'll realize that sixty years from now," said Grandma Lillian. Then she laughed without warning. "What are you going to do when I'm not here anymore? Who is going to answer all your questions?"

I told her that I was counting on her being around for a long time yet—at least another thirty years—although I knew that this was wishful thinking. Soon enough the slaughter of the Latvian Jews will be only a second-hand memory, as unlikely to draw an emotional response from anyone as a visit to Blanche at the nursing home. That is the horror of the past: that it is so expansive, and remote, and each day it expands exponentially, tearing through the emotional threads that bind it to the present. Already Blanche is not Blanche, but merely somebody's mother, grandmother, ex-girlfriend. Already the man who was not my grandfather is only that, and nothing more. When I am gone, he will be nothing at all.

Caesura—Antwerp, 1938

My grandparents came from remarkably different worlds, yet their relationship thrived for sixty-five years because they agreed about nearly everything. In the first months of their marriage, of course, they'd endured the occasional squabble. My grandfather, whose Orthodox Jewish family had fled Belgium ahead of the Nazis, adjusted slowly to the idea of his wife shopping in short sleeves and slacks, while my secular, Brooklyn-born grandmother saw little benefit from a Sabbath morning squandered at synagogue, but over the years Grandpa Leo's Judaism lapsed into the High Holiday variety while in return Grandma Lillian tolerated joining him for services at the Jewish Center two days each year. On other matters, no daylight shined between them: they enjoyed the same meals (McDonald's coffee, fried fish at the Nautilus Diner), embraced the same pastimes (canasta, game shows, people-watching at the county mall), voted for the same candidates (always Democrats), and complained of the same in-laws. They strove to outdo each other in both their extreme financial caution and their generosity toward their children and grandchildren. As they grew older, their bodies even shrank at the same rate. However, there was one subject concerning which their styles and philosophies never merged: wristwatches.

Grandpa Leo was a jeweler by profession—he'd run his own shop before it went belly-up in the 1950s—and he'd trained in the fine art of setting gemstones and ornamenting precious metals in the bustling workshops of prewar Antwerp. His adolescent friends had been aspiring goldsmiths, engravers, watchmakers; his younger sister, my aunt Paula, apprenticed as a diamond cutter. On his list of heroes, ranking behind only the great Jewish-European triad of Dreyfus and Herzl and Weizmann, towered businessmen such as Max Fischer, who presided over Antwerp's celebrated jewelry emporiums. So for my grandfather, who could dismantle and reassemble the most intricate timepiece, sporting a fine mechanical watch was a matter of both pride and distinction. That didn't mean he'd throw away money on a luxury timepiece by Breitling or Cartier, even if he'd been able to afford one, which he couldn't, but simply that he valued a watch that could be relied on and that did its job with precision. In contrast, my grandmother, accustomed to dipping her swollen arms into clogged washing machines and tins of cake batter, wanted a device that she could damage without regret. To this day she still wears the discount model that she purchased years ago at a variety shop; she may be the last living person who regularly replaces a three-dollar battery on a five-dollar analog watch.

All this matters, or at least matters to me, because approximately ten years ago, while on vacation in Spain, my grandfather's watch stopped abruptly. I was not with Grandpa Leo at the time—I was ensconced at medical school in New York City—yet this minor chronometric setback proved a transformative moment in our relationship.

My grandparents had been spending their winters in Torremolinos, on Spain's Costa del Sol, since the early 1980s; prior to that they'd passed October through March of each year on the Canary Islands, where they'd narrowly missed the Tenerife Airport Disaster of 1977 by a matter of days. What my grandfather enjoyed most about both the Canaries and the Spanish Riviera was the influx of Dutch and Flemish pensioners with whom he could speak in his mother tongue. He'd also strike up conversations with British and French and even German tourists in their native languages. My grandmother, who'd grown up speaking Yiddish, managed to follow the German. In a decade of winters, neither of my grandparents had learned a word of Spanish.

Each visit my grandparents stayed at the same hotel, joined the same couples for cards after dinner at the same buffet, and made the same bus excursion to Gibraltar, where they smuggled the same wine and cigars back into Spain for the same English friends. Only this year, while strolling on the boardwalk, my grandfather checked his watch—and found the hands frozen in time. To a man who prized both his time and his timepiece, this proved a more significant frustration than it might have been to the average octogenarian vacationer. Under the circumstances, I imagine, most individuals would have purchased a new watch—at least to tide them over until they could return to the United States to have the original repaired. Instead Grandpa Leo dissected the apparatus like a skilled surgeon and soon identified the cause of the malfunction. He now knew what the problem was and he knew how to fix it. All that he lacked was the tiny piece of silver required to replace the damaged wheel.

Unfortunately watch repair is a dying craft. While many shops in Torremolinos could sell my grandfather a new watch, none stocked *parts* for watches. What would be the purpose? Anyone with a watch expensive enough to qualify for repair could easily afford to send the device back to its manufacturer in Germany or Switzerland for a tune-up. The proletarian masses possessed the common sense to discard a broken watch and to invest in a cheap replacement. Eventually, after making inquiries of various mâitre d's and hotel ombudsmen, my grandparents learned that in a "neighboring" village, a two-hour bus ride up a dusty hillside, a wrinkled foreigner, who sold costume jewelry, also had experience repairing watches. So the following morning, Grandpa Leo and Grandma Lillian set out on a twenty-euro excursion to purchase a one-euro gear.

Grandpa Leo found far more than his missing sliver of metal in that dusty Spanish village: it turned out that the last watch repairman on the Costa del Sol had been my grandfather's boyhood friend in Antwerp. Each man had assumed the other was long dead. They shook hands, then they hugged; then they spoke Flemish at a rapid clip while my grandmother stood alongside them, befuddled, probably feeling like she did in synagogue. The two jewelers had Grandpa's watch working within minutes.

And that was that. The elderly watch repairman hadn't been my grandfather's long-lost brother; my grandfather hadn't been searching for him. This is not one of those Holocaust memoirs where two soul mates reunite after half a century and reminisce over how life might have developed if not for the Nazi genocide. No, this story is quite the opposite—the elderly watch repairman had been a good friend of my grandfather's in the 1930s, but Grandpa Leo had claimed many good friends in those days. Neither man deluded himself that their encounter was anything more than a delightful but brief interlude.

In short my grandparents returned to New York City, shared the pleasant coincidence of the meeting with their family, and then never mentioned the watch repairman again. I don't even know the old man's name. My grandfather has been dead for nearly five years, so I cannot ask him, and my grandmother insists she doesn't remember.

The second half of my grandfather's story is well known to me: his arrival on the SS *Champlain* in 1938, his successful scramble to bring his elderly parents and younger sisters to the

United States before the outbreak of war, his successive moves up the homeowner's totem pole from struggling St. Albans to middle-class Lynbrook to comfortable Mamaroneck. I've heard countless times of his frustration when stranded atop a Coney Island ride with an obese date during a power failure; of how his World War II army buddies overturned a segregated bus in Anniston, Alabama, after the driver refused a seat to a pregnant black woman; about his forty-year argument with his sister over the cost of an electric dryer; about the time he ate a nonkosher bologna sandwich so as not to offend an impoverished host; and about his hare-brained plan to market "prescription windshields" to vision-impaired drivers. All of that I know well. But the first half of the story, of the years between 1919 and 1937, I know nearly nothing.

Not for want of asking. But whatever the question, the answer always proved hazy. My grandfather mentioned many "friends" and "mates," but I can never remember him identifying any of them by name. When pressed, he served up some Reaganesque shade of "I can't recall." My former girlfriend and I even drove down from her home in Holland to visit the address of Grandpa Leo's boyhood home in Antwerp's Jewish Quarter—a structure bombed flat during the war and replaced with an all-too-modern apartment building. The neighborhood still teems with the same ultra-Orthodox men in caftans and fur-rimmed *shtramels* whose forebears surrounded my teenage grandfather seven decades ago, the descendants of refugees from Poland and White Russia and my grandfather's own family village in Romania. Yet today it is nearly impossible to situate Grandpa Leo, so modern in his bow tie and business suit, among the tradition-bound men and women he left behind.

Here is what I do know of my grandfather's life in prewar Antwerp, in the twelve years between his arrival from the east and his departure to the west: he wore wooden shoes for yard work, he belonged to a Jewish youth group that took swimming trips to the Dutch resort of Scheveningen, and he was traumatized when his kid sister, my aunt Paula, fell headfirst off a balcony onto a stone courtyard and barely recovered. I also know that when he returned home from school each afternoon—a Catholic school where he was one of the only Jewish students—he'd have to race past the adjoining church, where gentile high-school students pelted him with stones and urged him to "Go back to Palestine!" (The first words of French *I* ever learned were *sale Juif.*) Later, after his brother-in-law died fighting for the Loyalists during the Spanish Civil War, Grandpa Leo read the writing on the geopolitical wall and followed his elder sister to the United States. That meant giving up his dreams of becoming a master jeweler or gem dealer and instead accepting a life far more modest and safe. And he accepted—a wise choice, in hindsight—and lived to very happy old age across the Atlantic.

Shortly after Grandpa Leo's death, my grandmother found a striking document stashed among his personal papers. It is a letter, in French, written from his cousin Marcel to his sister

Paula in late 1945. The text is short and to the point. It reads (in part) roughly: "We are here in Paris, and we are safe. Alas, the news from the East is not good. We have heard nothing of the following relatives, and we can only assume the worst." And what follows is a list—nearly two handwritten pages long—of names that none of my surviving family members can recognize.

Only when my grandfather told the story of his boyhood friend, over coffeecake and tea on my parents' veranda, did I finally realize what had always before been too obvious to recognize: all those other childhood friends, in the hazy stories that my grandfather did share, were dead—carried off by the occupying SS between 1940 and 1944. Everybody he'd known in prewar Antwerp, in fact, was dead, except for the handful of relatives who'd followed him to New York, and an elderly watch repairman perched on a dusty hilltop near the Spanish coast. For my grandfather, time had stopped like a broken watch in 1938 in Antwerp—and when it restarted in Manhattan, after a seven-day voyage across the Atlantic, it did so in a different continuum, its hours and minutes both identical to and entirely unlike the hours and minutes preceding his escape.

I now own my grandfather's watch. I don't actually possess it. My mother, as is her habit, secured it in one of the numerous cubbyholes and niches around her house in which she hides valuables—and at present she can't find it. (For years, she kept her jewelry in the kitchen freezer to deceive burglars, and I've always imagined a frustrated thief sitting down in her kitchen for a snack, after a futile ransacking of the premises, to find diamonds and emeralds pouring out of an ice cream carton.) It is a fine watch, needless to say, but not a particularly valuable one. I suspect that if my mother never finds it, the next owners of the house will likely discover it someday—tucked behind the dishwasher or taped beneath an attic vent. It will have stopped by then, obviously, after many years without attention. I can picture the owner experimenting with the knobs, winding the hands by trial and error, comparing the delicate machine to his own digital device and reflecting, "How differently they measured time in those days." He will be more right than he knows.

Sudden Death—A Eulogy

My great-grandfather Simon Litman, Latvian immigrant, secular Jew, inept businessman, gifted egg candler, doting father, cigar smoker, and pint-sized omnivore who (at least in family lore) could devour his own body weight in *gribenes,* holds the distinction of being the last of my forebears to drop dead. He made his dramatic exit on a balmy spring evening in 1950, strolling home with his wife from a Saturday supper at my grandmother's house in St. Albans, Queens. At the dinner table, he'd appeared in good health and good cheer. Nevertheless several blocks up the avenue, opposite a fire station, he told my great-grandmother, "I don't feel so good," then clutched one hand to his chest, fell to his knees, and stopped breathing. He was sixty years old. To this day my ninety-one-year-old grandmother remains livid that none of the firemen responded to her mother's cries for help. "They must have heard her," she says. "How could they not have heard her?" Of course, that was before defibrillators and vasopressors, an era when dropping dead was a natural part of life. If the entire fire department had arrived en masse with paramedics in tow, they'd have had nothing therapeutic to offer.

Six decades after Great-Grandpa Simon plunged off his mortal coil, sudden death now threatens to go the way of rotary telephones and passenger pigeons. The exact rate at which we are not dropping dead is difficult to calculate. While the government keeps meticulous records on the causes of our deaths, and the ages at which we perish, it makes no effort to estimate the speed of our grand finales. Nonetheless, as a physician, I'd hazard a guess that we're not dying nearly as suddenly as we once did. "When I started as an intern," an elderly colleague recently observed at a staff meeting, "most patients stayed in the hospital only for a day or two. Either you got better or you didn't. Lingering wasn't part of the protocol." Today, in contrast, lingering on our mortal coil is the norm. Your insurance company—not rigor mortis—forces you out of the hospital. Where a generation ago, the expectation was for men to retire at sixty-five and keel over at sixty-seven— the basis for the pension plans now bankrupting municipal governments—a massive myocardial infarction in one's fifth or sixth decade is no longer inevitable. Stress tests and statins and improved resuscitation methods mean we are more likely to survive to our second heart attack, live beyond our third stroke. Life ends with a whimper, not a bang.

That is not to say that the Grim Reaper *never* arrives on a bolt of lightning: I've lost a medical-school mentor to a plane crash, a neighbor to suicide, a childhood friend to a brain aneurysm. Thousands of Americans, smoking less but eating more, still do succumb to heart attacks in their fifties and sixties. But we greet these swift departures not only with grief, as we have always done, but also with a sense of indignation simmering toward outrage. In an age of prenatal genetic testing and full-body PET scans and rampant agnosticism, all varieties of death strike many of us as anathema. Death without fair warning becomes truly obscene.

Increasingly our first associations with "sudden death" are metaphorical. "Sudden death" terminates ice hockey games and World Cup matches, not the lives of our friends and relatives. Blair's, the condiment enterprise, has transformed "sudden death" into a flavor of hot sauce; music impresario Joey Keithley co-opted it for a punk record label. Some time ago I had the pleasure of seeing the singer Molly Hager in concert, a woman who embodies my—and many other men's—epitome of feminine beauty, and I made the mistake of observing to my date that Ms. Hager was "drop-dead gorgeous." My date replied, acidly, "in that case, keep staring." Needless to say, as forcefully as I ogled, my heart beat only faster; it did not stop. "Drop-dead gorgeous," of course, means far less in a world where people don't actually drop dead. (Insert a comma between "dead" and "gorgeous," and it sounds like a threat Humphrey Bogart might have served up to Lauren Bacall during a spat.) We can speak figuratively about sudden death, trivialize it—even joke about it—because we do not actually expect to confront it. Not now, not soon, not until we've been afforded ample time to prepare. And, with each new medical innovation, the odds are more likely that we won't.

My own family doctor has a sign on his office door that reads, "SUDDEN DEATH IS GOD'S WAY OF TELLING YOU TO SLOW DOWN." If that is indeed the case, God has been letting us accelerate with impunity for some time now.

In 1958 John Kenneth Galbraith's *Affluent Society* reminded Americans that, for the first time in human history, we lived in a civilization where a majority of people did not have to worry about basic subsistence. More than five decades later, we find ourselves belonging to the first civilization where sudden death is the glaring exception, not the expectation. The novelty of our position is all too easy to forget; it is even easier to assume without questioning that the present state of affairs reflects progress. After all, which of us wouldn't rather die well prepared at ninety than suddenly at fifty-five? And yet the more I see of death, the less convinced I become that, in this medical and social revolution, we have not lost something of considerable value. I certainly don't mean to glorify premature death: I suspect both "dying with one's boots on" and "living fast, loving hard, and dying young" are highly overrated feats. I do not believe that it is either *dulce* or *decorum* to die at twenty-five for one's country. My concern is also not with the economic effects of the long goodbye—the percent of Medicare dollars spent in the last six months of life, the prospect of every gainfully employed worker supporting two retirees. Rather, my disquiet is principally for lost human dignity. Canadian right-to-die activist Gloria Taylor, who suffers from Lou Gehrig's disease, recently wrote, "I can accept death because I recognize it as a part of life. What I fear is a death that negates, as opposed to concludes, my life." Sudden death is a conclusion. Too often, I fear, the long goodbye devolves into a negation.

The contrast between the death of my grandmother's father and that of her husband fifty-eight years later is highly revealing. Grandpa Leo, a Belgian refugee who earned a comfortable living in the jewelry business, developed prostate cancer in his early seventies, survived a mild heart attack at age seventy-seven, and by his mid-eighties had trouble remembering the names of his sisters. And then, at eighty-six, he developed a metastatic lesion on the surface of his brain. In 1950 the cancer would have killed him in a matter of months. In 2006 a skilled neurosurgeon managed to scoop out the bulk of the tumor, enabling my grandfather to survive to a series of small strokes a full year later. Once again, these cerebral insults—as the medical chart termed them—would certainly have ended an octogenarian's life in his own father-in-law's generation. But after a two-month-long hospital stay and tens of thousands of dollars in high-tech imaging, modern anticoagulants enabled Grandpa Leo to roll into a nursing home that he actually believed to be his mother's apartment in prewar Antwerp.

I visited him one afternoon, and he announced how much he loved his wife—but he was actually referring to the young

West African woman assigned to change his bed linens. It took two intubations, weeks on a ventilator, multiple courses of dialysis, and a month of unconsciousness before my grandmother finally cried uncle and brought the process of her husband's dying to a halt. By then the man I'd worshiped as a child for his vigor and independence had gone nearly a half a year without responding to his own name. When Grandpa Leo died—after the best nursing care imaginable—his entire torso had become one enormous bedsore, his back and shoulders assuming the color of a side of tenderized beef. Is my grandfather's longevity a triumph or a tragedy? On the one hand, I am grateful that I had an opportunity to know my grandfather well into my own adulthood—an opportunity that my father never had. On the other hand, faced with the prospect of following in my grandfather's footsteps, I'd much rather drop dead in front of a firehouse at sixty.

In medical ethics—the field in which I do my academic research and writing—the way we now die has led to the birth of entirely novel schools of thought. When life was truly brutish and short, whether in Hobbes's sixteenth-century London or Great-Grandpa Simon's mid-twentieth-century New York, the idealistic notion that all life was sacred and must be preserved at any cost carried limited weight in medical and moral circles. Although we have come to think of the modern era, post–Karen Ann Quinlan and Terri Schiavo, as one in which we tolerate excessive medical care less than in past generations, the reality is that physicians and patients were once much more accepting of death than they are now. They had to be. The so-called culture of life, so recently embraced by the Catholic Church and the Southern Baptist Convention, generally advances the view that life in its essence, rather than its quality, is of paramount value. The impact of this viewpoint on modern health care and medical discourse cannot be underestimated. Yet this dogma is far more a product of technology and material change than of theological evolution. In a world where it was more common for people to keel over on street corners without advance notice, the notion of controlling (or even defeating) death made little sense.

The slow demise of sudden death has also reshaped vast aspects of our culture and our iconography with little notice and less comment. How does it alter our society to live in a world influenced by elder statement—and then to watch those elder statesmen dotter into decrepitude? Franklin Roosevelt will forever be a jaunty sixty-three, Adlai Stevenson a distinguished sixty-five, Estes Kefauver—for those who still remember him—a scrappy sixty. In contrast, Ronald Reagan, as his memory faded and his world grew smaller, lost much of his magic. Clark Gable didn't lock in his permanent sex appeal as Rhett Butler or Fletcher Christian, but instead is also remembered as having a catastrophic thrombosis at fifty-nine. Nor is it clear in Marlon Brando's case that an extra two decades enhanced his legacy.

Whether these changes are beneficial or deleterious, they are likely irreversible—at least by rational planning. Needless to say, we can't ethically go around inducing cardiac arrests in healthy sixty-year-olds. What we can do—and what we have not been doing—is paying closer attention to the complex ways in which how we die is transforming how we live.

I fear the most subtle, yet most pernicious, consequence of a world in which people do not as often die suddenly is a world in which people do not appreciate life. My great-grandfather's favorite expression—one of the few memories remaining of him to the rapidly shrinking circle of old-timers who still remember his earthly presence at all—was, fittingly, "We're so lucky to be alive!" Great-Grandpa Simon uttered these words in Yiddish, of course; his limited English was reserved for essential business transactions with gentiles. And coursing through them was clearly not only an awareness of the vagaries of natural death, but also the threat of violent demise at the hands of his fellow human beings, the ever-fresh memory of his baby sisters and their families slaughtered by Nazi Einsatzgruppen in the Daugavpils ghetto. (Ironically and fittingly, a generation later, my Grandpa Leo's favorite expression was, "Where there's life, there's hope.") Today a brush with death often drives us to reexamine our lives, the starting point of many a popular movie and middle-age crisis. Half a century ago, men like my great-grandfather didn't require such a brush with death: living past fifty was itself enough of a risk to generate reflection and gratitude.

An Absence of Jell-O

Lime Jell-O, as served up in my grandaunt's kitchen, was a weapon of torture.

Among my earliest childhood memories are the three-hour drive along the backbone of Long Island to the cozy, tchotchke-cluttered home of my mother's aunt and uncle, Eddie and Shirley Sadowsky, who had escaped the Jewish ghetto of the Bronx for the tidy uniformity of suburban Patchogue. My uncle had earned his living in the tire business. In his youth he'd been quite the ladies' man—he was already divorced when he married into my mother's family, an unspeakable blemish for the suitor of a respectable girl in the 1920s—but by the time I knew him, he had mellowed into an irascible geezer who passed his retirement in petty warfare with his sisters-in-law. My aunt had once been damaged goods too, her neck disfigured by a savage scar from where her thyroid gland had been extracted in her teens. Since she died when I was only nine, I recall little of Aunt Shirley, a soft-featured woman who concealed both her hair and her throat beneath a cloak of faded *schmattas*. What I do remember vividly is her greeting me in the foyer, amid the swirl of hugging and hanging of coats, and whispering into my five- or six- or seven-year-old ear that there was to be Jell-O for dessert—*if I behaved!* I was not to tell anyone, warned my aunt. The Jell-O was to be our secret.

That Jell-O was to be spoken of in hushed tones—like divorce or cancer—was not shocking to me at that age. My parents kept a strictly kosher home. They didn't distinguish between the trace of porcine collagen in gelatin-based desserts and procuring a ham-and-cheese sandwich or a suckling pig. Not that I didn't know the nirvana of Jell-O firsthand: my mother's stepmother, who had little patience for arbitrary doctrine, took a sly pleasure in treating me to *trayf* delicacies. At Aunt Shirley's house, however, I never managed to behave well enough to earn my slurpy, sugary reward. Sometimes I tried to prolong our stay, feigning sleep or even illness, hoping that my aunt would find a way to sneak me a spoonful of my favorite snack. Inevitably, though, I left Patchogue with an empty stomach and a soul brimming with dejection. Another ten years would pass before I realized that there had never been any lime Jell-O. My grandaunt had been senile, demented, soft-in-the-head. Today we'd say she suffered from Alzheimer's disease, but, for my working-class relatives in the 1970s, Aunt Shirley's mental lapses were just an expected and unpleasant part of growing old.

Pythagoras of Samos, writing in the sixth century before Christ, described old age as the time when people "return to the imbecility of the first epoch of infancy." Chaucer lamented that "with old folk, save dotage, is namore," while Dickens captured the essence of cognitive decline in his sympathetic portrait of "The Aged P" in *Great Expectations*. Although the German neuropathologist Alois Alzheimer first reported in 1906 the disease that would take his name, describing the ailment's distinctive amyloid plaques and neurofibrillary tangles in the preserved brain of housewife Auguste Deter, and Emil Kraepelin included the condition in an edition of his *Textbook of Psychiatry* in 1910, senile dementia was widely regarded as a normal variant of the aging process into the early 1980s. Patients suffered without a formal clinical diagnosis, often alone, although sometimes very publicly, as the actress Rita Hayworth did for nearly fifteen years. Nobody knew what caused the accumulation of deformed proteins in the brains of some senior citizens, while others lived into their eighties and nineties with minds as sharp as talons. When Uncle Eddie asked his family physician *why* his wife was having difficulty recalling names and recognizing faces, he received an answer that reflected cutting-edge Carter-era neurology: "Bad luck."

As a result of the genetic revolution of the last two decades, we now know that much of the "bad luck" that causes Alzheimer's disease is mediated by our genes. In particular one locus on chromosome 19, the apoliprotein E, or ApoE, gene, is highly implicated in the risk for senile dementia. This gene comes in three allelic variants: ApoE-2, ApoE-3, and ApoE-4. Since a child inherits one allele from each parent, an adult's DNA can contain any of six different combinations at the ApoE site: E-2/E-2, E-2/E-3, E-2/E-4, E-3/E-3, E-3/E-4, or E-4/E-4. The majority of human beings, somewhere between 50 and 65 percent of us, are double E-3s. This is considered to be the "neutral" or baseline variant with regard to Alzheimer's disease. Compared to double E-3s, the quarter of us who carry an E-3/E-4 combination are approximately four times as likely to develop Alzheimer's disease in old age. A smaller minority of us, somewhere between 1 and 3 percent, are double E-4s and are therefore *fifteen* times as susceptible to the disorder. Yet genetic prediction is not yet an exact science, and it turns out that not *all* double E-4s eventually lose their minds. A fortunate subset of double E-4s, for reasons yet unknown, remains lucid into the ninth and tenth decades. Of course, some centenarians also chain smoke and drink heavily, but these folks prove to be the exceptions—and while you can quit smoking, you cannot (for now, at least) alter your genetic makeup. So while carrying one of two E-4 alleles is not an automatic death sentence, like harboring a gene for Huntington's chorea, it is certainly a cause for concern.

When Aunt Shirley was my age—in 1932—medicine had no method for unraveling a person's genetic code. Predicting the likelihood of senile dementia was a matter for clairvoyants, not scientists. Today, in contrast, any one of dozens of direct-to-consumer companies will determine your ApoE makeup. You send them a cheek swab or saliva sample and several hundred dollars, they run a laboratory test, and four weeks later you learn whether you're a double E-3, an E-4/E-3, or a double E-4. The genetic revolution has made such revelation *possible*. Whether a person *wants* to discover his or her susceptibility for Alzheimer's disease is another matter entirely.

People who contemplate learning their ApoE susceptibility must grapple with the rather striking fact that several of the strongest advocates for personal genomics have chosen not to learn their Alzheimer's risk. In an essay in the *New York Times Magazine* in 2009, Harvard-based evolutionary psychologist Steven Pinker—who has become for the brain what Carl Sagan was for the cosmos—explained that when his DNA was surveyed by the Personal Genome Project, he requested a "line-item veto" of his ApoE status. Pinker followed the lead of the molecular biologist James Watson, codiscoverer (with Francis Crick) of the structure of DNA, who more than any other living human being is responsible for the technology that makes such testing possible. Pinker wrote that "All of us already have a fatal genetic condition called mortality, and most of us cope using some combination of denial, resignation and religion." He added that he found his "current burden of existential dread" to be "just about right" without knowing his ApoE results. I recall reading Pinker's article as I was contemplating the possibility of investigating my own ApoE information and

wondering if these geniuses don't want to know their susceptibility to Alzheimer's disease, why would I?

The question runs much deeper than memory loss. What
genetic testing forces a person to decide is whether or not he
or she desires to know the future—or, at least, statistical likeli-
hoods regarding that future. Would you want to learn that as
you approach your seventies or eighties, you will start to lose
your grasp on the details of your childhood? That common
words will grow harder to find? Well-known faces less familiar?
That while your spouse is wondering where her keys are, you'll
be wondering what your keys do? Of course, genetic testing
can also reveal the very opposite—a reduced risk of memory
loss, the reassurance that one will likely remember the trials
and tribulations of youth into the extremes of age.

While Professor Pinker is forgoing an opportunity to
increase his existential dread, he is also sacrificing a chance
to reduce it. To see this choice more clearly, one can imagine
the ethical conundrum that a hypothetical transatlantic pilot
might face on learning that a bomb was to detonate aboard the
fully booked aircraft in fifteen minutes, ensuring the instant
deaths of all the passengers. Ought the pilot announce his
discovery over the public-address system in order to let the
passengers use their final moments as they wish? This would
enable the doomed passengers to pray, or possibly to send
text messages to their families—but it might also increase
their suffering significantly. The alternative—keeping them
in the dark—would decrease both their autonomy and their

distress. Now complicate this scenario by changing the certainty that the bomb is aboard the plane from 100 to 25 percent. Should the pilot tell his passengers that there is a 25 percent chance that they will die in fifteen minutes? Similarly, whether Pinker or I learn our ApoE status has absolutely no bearing on whether we will develop Alzheimer's disease. All the test determines is whether we might suffer through knowledge or perish in ignorance. With genetic testing, however, everyone becomes the pilot.

If deciding to learn your own ApoE status already seems difficult enough, it is rendered all the more challenging because in unveiling your own genetic makeup, you can inadvertently unmask the genes of your relatives. Let us say, for example, that I were to discover that I carried a double whammy: two ApoE-4s. That would mean that each of my parents carried at least one E-4—making them roughly four times more likely than the average person to develop Alzheimer's disease. Even if I carried only a single E-4, this might still prove revealing, as these findings do not occur in a vacuum. Nobody in my father's family dating back to the nineteenth century, as far as I know, has ever suffered from Alzheimer's disease. My mother, on the other hand, has no siblings, and neither of her parents lived to seventy, but she has an aunt with unquestionable dementia. The combination of one E-4 and a maternal grand-aunt with memory loss would be strong—although not conclusive—indicators that the undesired variant had come from my mother. Yet my mother, I am confident, has no desire to learn her risk. Her own mother died of breast cancer when my mother was eight years old, but she has never had a mammogram. Why not? Because, she has explained, "If I had a mammogram, I might find out that I have cancer." I cannot fathom she'd want to discover she was ApoE-4 positive. My results also have implications for my brother, my cousins, and—if I ever choose to have them—my own children, who may learn their fates from my genes.

However, that is the complexity of modern genomics. At the end of this essay, I reveal my ApoE status. In theory, that status can affect my aunt Shirley's other grandnieces and grandnephews—none of whom I know personally. If several of us collateral relatives united to reveal our variants or collaborated with other relatives of those grandnieces and grandnephews, we could go a long way toward exposing the status of family members who wished their fate to remain cloaked in existential darkness. In some cultures, that knowledge might then affect people's choice of mate or opportunities to have biological children. Although the Genetic Information Nondiscrimination Act of 2008 prevents potential employers and health insurers from bias based on a person's genetic makeup, the reality is that when your boss knows that you are likely to lose your mind, you may be treated differently.

Recognizing all of this, I still decided to be tested. Why? A part of my desire was sheer curiosity—much as I might choose to learn my anticipated date of death, if that knowledge were ever to become available. But I confess I was also gambling, hoping that I might win the genetic lottery and reduce my existential dread. I suppose I should admit here that I am also not an ordinary participant in the genetic lottery. I am a professional bioethicist and an outspoken advocate for assisted suicide. If I do develop Alzheimer's disease, I am resolutely determined to put a bullet through my temple. Understanding my risk is certain to make me more attuned to the signs of the ailment, less likely to end my life prematurely if I cannot remember where I placed my glasses. My worst fear is not knowing that I will die prematurely, or even at my own hand, but the prospect of torturing my future grandnephews and grandnieces with false promises of lime Jell-O. Aunt Shirley could not help how she ended up. To the extent that I can, I am determined to try.

Deciding to test one's ApoE variant is only half the battle. Thanks to a New York State Department of Health run amok, such testing is now illegal where I live. Or, to be more precise, it's illegal without preauthorization from a physician. The great irony of this is that I am a physician and an authority on genetic ethics, but I would still have to convince my own primary-care provider to persuade my insurer that the test is "medically indicated"—which it assuredly is not—when, if I lived elsewhere, I could simply send my $200 to a direct-to-consumer start-up at substantially less cost to either me or the health-care system. I suppose the state's concern is that uninformed individuals might learn their ApoE status and immediately jump off the George Washington Bridge in despair. (The reality, according to a study by Robert Green, is that people who learn they are ApoE positive accept the discouraging results and continue on with their lives.) To circumvent these rules, I had to establish residency in the state of Massachusetts, which I did for a period of several hours, in order to foil the efforts of the nanny state. I swabbed my cheek and had my results sent to a temporary address across the border. I'd like to think of myself as a modern-day Joe Kennedy, running bootleg DNA, but the arguments for preventing people from charting their own genetic makeup cause alcohol prohibition to seem comparatively sensible. I can think of no other enterprise in which the authorities believe the lay public is better served with less information, rather than more.

The direct-to-consumer company I chose for my ApoE assessment takes approximately six weeks to deliver its results. Twice, during my wait, I nearly canceled the test. Both times, I convinced myself that the promise of good news was worth the risk of bad results. I didn't inform my mother that I had sent my DNA to a laboratory in California, but I couldn't resist quizzing her about Aunt Shirley and her final years. When had my grandaunt first showed signs of dementia? How had the family reacted? Did anybody else in the family have similar symptoms? Needless to say, my mother found these inquiries suspicious. Her aunt had been dead for twenty-seven years, after all, and neither of us had ever been particularly close to her. When I explained that I was writing an essay on Alzheimer's disease, my mother flashed a peculiar frown. She was seated at the kitchen table, sipping tea in her bathrobe, a woman closer in age to the elderly grandaunt I remembered from Patchogue than the young mother who had driven us to see her. "To tell you the truth," said my mother, "we've always said Shirley had Alzheimer's, but I'm not so sure. Honestly, she was *always* confused and forgetful, even when I was a little girl. It just got worse when she grew older." So my grandaunt, who had spurred me to test my genes for Alzheimer's disease, likely didn't have it. "Even when I was a little girl," continued my mother, "Shirley used to offer everyone Jell-O. It didn't matter whether she actually had any Jell-O. She'd offer it anyway. We shrugged it off at the time. That was just Aunt Shirley being Aunt Shirley. But if you want my personal opinion, I think that thyroid surgery she had as a kid addled her brain."

"*Jell-O?*" I asked incredulously. "She offered you *Jell-O?*"

"Nobody talked about these sorts of things back then," answered my mother. "It's amazing what you realize about people when it no longer matters."

Two weeks later, my ApoE results arrived. After all my efforts to establish a dummy postal address elsewhere, they appeared in my email box: one file containing my results and another explaining what they meant—including a disclaimer that susceptibility for Alzheimer's disease is not a guarantee of getting it. Before I opened the fateful file, I went to the refrigerator and removed the cup of lime Jell-O I'd been saving for the occasion. Somehow this seemed like a fitting tribute to my late grandaunt, who may or may not have suffered from Alzheimer's disease. When I'd scooped the last slurp of gelatin from the cup, I steeled myself and clicked on the file:

ApoE-3 ApoE-3

I am a double ApoE-3. I have won my genetic gamble. My risk of developing Alzheimer's disease is no higher than that of a random person chosen from the phonebook—likely somewhat lower, once those with ApoE-4 alleles are subtracted. Yet my risk is not zero either. It is not even particularly low. Just a tad below average. I suppose my burden of existential dread is somewhat lighter, but I am not entirely sure; maybe the weight is just distributed differently. What I really want, of course, is not to know why Aunt Shirley offered me lime Jell-O or what my cognitive future holds. What I really want is for there *to be* lime Jell-O, for that five- and six- and seven-year-old boy who behaved so well, dreaming of a treat that will never come. How long does it take, I wonder, for a grown man with two ApoE-3 alleles to forget an absence of Jell-O?

She Loves Me Not

Unrequited love again. This time it's an up-and-coming jazz singer who works in a pet shop. Even *I* am surprised that I've fallen for her. My penchant is for dark-eyed girls with full breasts and child-bearing hips, sturdy women bearing Mediterranean or Slavic surnames. If I were placed in charge of selecting *Playboy* Bunnies and *Penthouse* Pets—and I don't anticipate being hired anytime soon—all the centerfolds would resemble the title heroine in *My Ántonia*. Yet the current object of my affections—let's call her Kate*—is about as far from Willa Cather's Bohemian beauty as New York City is from Red Cloud, Nebraska. She's slight. She's flat-chested.

---

*Any personal essay on "unrequited love" that discusses real people runs the risk of causing substantial discomfort and emotional pain to the friends and family of the author. I have altered several details in this narrative—very minor matters of geography, occupation, and genealogy—in order to protect the identities and

No industrial detergent could bleach her cheeks or eyebrows any paler. When I first met her, at a sleepy café in the West Village, love didn't enter my mind. It was money, rather, that brought us together—she had accidentally walked off with *my* change. Only later, after I'd somehow blundered my way into conversation, did I topple headfirst for Kate's beguiling laughter. Hers is a high-pitched, buttery laugh that coincides with a toss of her hair. It often follows confessions of deficiency, such as "I'm totally broke" or "I'm congenitally dishonest." If she'd said, "I axe-murdered my grandmother" or "I volunteer for a consortium of war criminals," the laugh might still have redeemed her.

Alas I am not Kate's sole admirer. She is engaged to marry a public defender who looks strikingly like Gregory Peck and who seems as genial and charismatic as Atticus Finch in *To Kill a Mockingbird.* There are rumors that he speaks both French and Mandarin fluently. (Although I've also studied some French—with Mme. Kaufman in eighth grade—I am not feeling bold enough to test him.) Mr. Truth-Justice-and-the-American-Way, his betrothal notwithstanding, is not my only competition. I'm fairly confident that the girl of my dreams has also been enjoying a *liaison* (note the French!) with a well-to-do architect with whom she takes capoeira lessons. I am not sure whether this second relationship is to my advantage.

---

feelings of the people involved. I have made such substitutions only in cases where failure to do so would have caused unnecessary harm and where doing so had no impact on the substance of the text.

While cluttering the playing field, it also suggests a certain instability in Kate's long-term plans. *I* am all about long-term planning. The calendar is the unrequited lover's principal ally. Divorce rates stand at over 50 percent, after all, probably higher among aspiring jazz singers. Even Rome fell eventually. Another essential factor, I've discovered, is determination. The trick is to desire a romantic relationship with Kate more than she *doesn't* desire one with me.

Over the years, while my friends have mastered accounting and journalism and dentistry, I've become something of an old pro at unrequited love. It is my niche, my field of expertise. Distinguishing "the genuine article" from a mere crush or transient infatuation is admittedly a thorny and subjective enterprise, but I can confidently stake my claim to a half-dozen unrequited love affairs. Over the past decade—in addition to my current pursuit—these have included a country-club waitress (six months), an amateur filmmaker (seven months), a professional tutor (ten months), a college undergraduate majoring in applied mathematics (one year), and an evolutionary biologist (two years plus). During this same period, I've enjoyed six requited romances—several of considerable duration. (I have made no effort to ascertain how many men and women have *loved me* unrequitedly during this interval, both because of the difficulty obtaining such data and also because the damage this figure might inflict on my ego.) How do the requited and unrequited loves compare? It would be easy to offer some glib assessment such as "rejection sucks eggs." Or, as Charlie Brown explains most eloquently, "Nothing takes the taste out of peanut butter quite like unrequited love." To a certain extent, of course, this wisdom is incontestable. Rejection *does* suck eggs. But this cannot be the full story. If unrequited love were so universally unrewarding, akin to touching a sizzling stove, even fools like me would learn to avoid it.

I recently discovered that I hail from a long line of unrequited lovers. My father pined for six months before securing a date with my mother. My great-grandfather stood outside my great-grandmother's tenement, day after day, week after week, until she finally agreed to marry him. According to family lore, one granduncle waited years for his true love's husband to die before confessing his pent-up affections—though take this tale with a grain of salt, because another version has them poisoning the husband together. But it is my mother's second cousin—let's call him Nathan Green—who is unquestionably our family's most devoted and hapless romantic.

Nathan is now in his eighties. Never married. Without children. Recently retired from a very successful psychiatry practice on the West Coast. He is classy, charismatic, and *still* eye-catchingly handsome. I have seen photographs of my cousin in his youth: shirtless at Cape May and Jones Beach, posing with his buddies in their midshipman uniforms. We are a family of round-shouldered welterweights, and yet, by our standards, Nathan's physique could have launched a thousand ships. (If I had been endowed with his perfectly chiseled Roman features, there's no telling what I might have done with my country-club waitress, amateur filmmaker, professional tutor, math major, or evolutionary biologist.) As it turned out, the only ship launching my cousin ever did was in the navy. My mother has known Nathan for more than half a century. He has shared our Passover seders and sent postcards from his extensive travels in Asia and Latin America. During that entire time, she cannot remember his going on one single date. He has always been chronically single, evolving through the years from "prized catch" to "confirmed bachelor." My private suspicion was that he frequented bars on Castro Street and enjoyed discreet encounters with other men—or possibly *one* relationship with *one* man—but I kept this hunch to myself.

My hunch proved wildly inaccurate. Visiting Nathan earlier this year in his California retirement community, my mother was taken aback by an "enormous" black-and-white photograph displayed "prominently" in his living room. She did not recognize its subject: a "stunningly beautiful" young woman. ("It didn't belong," Mom recalled. "It was like those vintage photographs that hang in chain restaurants.") Nathan explained that this stunningly beautiful young woman had recently passed away as a stunningly *unmarried* old woman. Unmarried—despite Nathan's numerous proposals. He'd moved halfway across the continent to be near her.* Fearing religious differences might impede their relationship, he'd converted to Catholicism. He'd even sanitized his name from the conspicuously Semitic to the ethnically neutral. Nothing worked. I can picture him inviting her to his dinner parties—thrown solely

---

*I never learned her real name—so a pseudonym seems inappropriate.

to lure her across town—and then following her from book-lined room to book-lined room, his heartstrings fluttering with her every breath. That is how I imagine it. All I can surmise about their relationship is that it waxed and waned over time, ranging from unspoken tension to warm camaraderie—but remained wholly platonic.* So Nathan waited . . . and waited . . . and waited. Years. Decades. Half a century. Approaching the twilight of his life, my cousin still adores this woman with all the intensity of a smitten teenager.

I've shared Nathan's story with a wide swath of my friends—everyone from academic psychiatrists to quixotic poets with melancholy temperaments. The response has been nearly uniform: "Loopy." "Bonkers." "Totally fucked up." Several female colleagues also found his behavior pathetic and a bit creepy. None of these dozens of critics lauded my relative's devotion as romantic or noble or majestically tragic. Nor did the poets rush to compose elegies in praise of his passion. The closest anyone came to an epic tribute was the suggestion that I send the tale to *Reader's Digest* as a novelty item. Almost my entire social circle thought the story bizarre and Nathan's "love" many standard deviations from the mean. A few also found the matter infuriating. One individual even snapped, "He got what he deserved." I was surprised by my friends' anger and angered by my friends' surprise. The world had

* I am relatively confident of this, although it is not the sort of question one can pose directly. If any romantic intimacy ever did occur between them, it was a phenomenon of the distant past.

clearly changed since my great-grandfather lingered under my great-grandmother's window. On the Lower East Side in 1890, that was considered courtship. Now it borders on stalking.*

Why have I related my cousin's story in such detail? Because its basic framework should feel uncannily familiar—at least to the vast majority of American high school graduates. A young man is jilted by his lover. After an interval of many years, he moves halfway across the country in hot pursuit. He constructs a house opposite hers and attempts to lure her with lavish parties. And he waits . . . and waits . . . and waits. Somewhere along the line he has even altered his name. In my family that name is Nathan Green. To F. Scott Fitzgerald, of course, it was Jay Gatsby. I concede my cousin's wait endured far longer than Gatsby's. Making too much of that— to my mind—sells Gatsby short. You have to take away the speeding yellow roadster. Take away Myrtle's fatal wave. Take away George Wilson and his handgun. What remains? A man who might easily wait half a century for the woman he loves. Loopy? Bonkers? Totally psychotic? I don't know. I've never once heard *The Great Gatsby* referred to as the "Great American Stalking Novel."

---

*I do not intend to diminish or make light of the seriousness of nonconsensual stalking, a form of intense harassment that often leads to violence. To me this is far different from courtship efforts such as my great-grandfather's, in which the suit is neither accepted nor denied, but allowed to linger in a state of persistent ambiguity. I certainly see no connection between criminal stalking and consensual friendships in which one party is motivated by unexpressed romantic sentiments for the other.

When it comes to unrequited love, we have a double standard. Our literature and films glorify behavior that we reject in real life as unbalanced or antisocial. I've heard *Gone with the Wind* criticized on numerous political and aesthetic grounds—and I sympathize with many of these assessments—but never once have I heard Scarlett's pursuit of Ashley Wilkes described as pathologic.

In Gabriel García Márquez's *Love in the Time of Cholera,* Florentino Ariza waits fifty-one years for Fermina Daza's husband to die so that he may continue the interrupted romance of their youth. I recently taught this enchanting novel in a college literature course. Most of my students heartily endorsed Florentino's constancy. The consensus was "Super sweet." One girl publicly announced that—if Florentino were to step off the printed page and into Washington Square Park—she'd gladly sleep with him. Another acknowledged sobbing at his plight. I did not hear one whispered allusion to borderline personalities or restraining orders. Nor did the docent on my tour of Theodore Roosevelt's Oyster Bay mansion suggest lunacy when she hinted that T.R.'s second wife, his childhood sweetheart, had been waiting in the wings for the death of his first.

How different from the plight of Mary B. She was an elderly acquaintance of my grandmother's, one of her Scrabble companions, who had been ditched while en route to the altar.* This misfortune dated back to the prewar era. 1925?

* According to my mother's secondhand account, Mary B. was "left at the altar"; I do not know whether this was merely a euphemism for a broken engagement or

1930? Mary B. never recovered. For five decades she shuffled from one forlorn residence to another with her two spinster sisters. I do not know to what degree, if any, she kept in touch with the departed suitor. I do know he married someone else and raised a family. (As the French say in France: *C'est la vie.*) And then—nearly fifty years later—he phoned her: "My wife passed on. Can I interest you in dinner?" We speak of this second-round romance as peculiar, comic, downright Dickensian. Nobody ever says, "Super sweet."* Over the past several months, as word has spread that I am writing an essay on unrequited love, I've discovered that stories like Nathan's and Mary B.'s are far more common than I had imagined. All sorts of people have crawled out of the woodwork to tell me about maiden aunts and bachelor uncles long languishing from unreciprocated affection. These loves frequently share motifs: family opposition, class differences, intervening military service—and reams and reams of correspondence. Others defy all expectations: a stranger in a coffee shop told me that his grandfather had waited for his grandmother to die so that he could marry her sister. Yet I was continually impressed with the unfaltering loyalty of the unrequited lovers. Making allowances for some exaggeration here and a bit of padding there, some of these relationships still survived longer than

---

if she was truly abandoned within a stone's throw of the baptismal font. All the parties are dead now; there is no longer anyone to ask.

*Mary B. and the widower married within months. They were divorced in less than two years. Maybe that says it all.

many marriages. So much for the theory that my family is unusual, that we carry a recessive "unrequited love" gene! It is possible, of course, that this anecdotal sampling is unrepresentative: that unrequited lovers are drawn to each other like lepidopterists and polka aficionados. (When taking Dutch lessons in college, I was amazed to find all of Boston teeming with Dutch speakers.) In my gut I suspect the opposite. Unrequited love, in a society that stigmatizes one-sided passion, is most likely an *underreported* phenomenon. We have no way of knowing how many hapless romantics, suffering like my cousin Nathan, carry their secrets to the grave.

So why do some of us love unrequitedly? "Because we can't help it." But that is a cop-out. Blaming unrequited love on irrepressible obsession is like attributing the misfortunes of King Lear to preordained dementia. Love is a choice. We *can* help it. We *choose* not to. If we truly couldn't help it, from my perspective, it wouldn't be love.

One theory of nonmutual attachment insists that unrequited lovers relish the exquisite suffering of rejection. As Dryden observed in *Tyrannic Love,* "Pains of love be sweeter far than all the other pleasures are." Maybe, up to a point. I'll admit I've indulged in more than my fair share of narcissistic wallowing and teenage masochism. But heartbreak hurts. Physically hurts. As much as a toothache or a broken rib. No acute sorrow, not even the death of a friend, can compare with romantic rejection. Such intense agony may be irrational— but, by definition, emotions aren't rational. So how are we to believe that Apollo *subconsciously* relishes his pursuit of

Daphne? That *deep down* Ophelia wants Hamlet to ignore her? I have my doubts. Rather, I subscribe to an opposing theory that claims we love unrequitedly because unrequited love *always* meets our expectations. In that regard romantic relationships resemble artistic creations. Gazing at the unsullied page—before I've scribbled my first words—my narrative is assuredly destined for *The Best American Essays*. Ready to take its rightful place beside the contributions of Jonathan Swift and Virginia Woolf and Thomas Jefferson. I sense the adrenaline gushing. This is *the one*. Unfortunately, then I start writing. . . .

Is it any different with love? As long as my dream girl keeps me at arm's length, I can still aspire to a perfect relationship. *Nobody* is perfect after the third date. By then I am under the sway of my own insecurities—the same tendency that leads me to denigrate the journals publishing my work and, à la Groucho, to reject country clubs willing to take me as a member. This is the tragicomic paradox: requited love will inexorably come up short. So I delude myself into believing, as the late Dag Hammarskjöld once mused for the world, "Perhaps a great love is never returned."

My own longest unrequited relationship is a study in Orwellian doublethink. I spent several years thoroughly devoted to an ecologist who analyzes lobster populations in New England. Ariana—yes, another pseudonym—ranks among the planet's spectacular human beings (though admittedly not as spectacular as I once fantasized). She is compassionate, generous, magical with children and animals. Unfortunately she would sooner drink hemlock than hold my hand. I chose not to know this. I was so consciously determined not to know this, so resolved to reshuffle the deck of fate, that for her birthday I bought her a copy of Somerset Maugham's *Of Human Bondage*. This led to long, abstract talks about Philip Carey's one-sided attachment to Mildred. I took *his* side. She took *hers*. We pretended they had nothing to do with us. Later I also contributed Proust and Galsworthy to her library. Nothing worked. No hoping. No praying. No negotiating with a higher power. And then—without warning—Ariana suffered a stroke. *What were the odds of a healthy young woman in her mid-twenties suffering a cerebral hemorrhage?!** Surely, this was my miracle. I visited the hospital every day. I brought flowers. I ran errands. My motives—if you're wondering—were both mixed and honorable. I wanted her to recover, *and* I wanted her to love me. Not goals in any way mutually exclusive. Much more time had to pass for me to learn Philip Carey's lesson: even blind and paralyzed, this woman was *never* going to love me.[†]

Which brings us back to Kate. The jazz singer from the café. I could write about her for a long eternity—her baking skills, her asymmetrical ears, her tortuous but side-splitting disquisitions on Bastille Day and grapefruit—but I won't do that.

* For the record: approximately 1 in 50,000.

† I am thrilled to say that Ariana's recovery has been as miraculous as her collapse was improbable. She once again sees like a hawk and hikes through the Andes.

I'm in love with her. You're not. I'll keep it brief.

Kate and I have become relatively close friends over the last half-year. I go to her concerts. I shake hands with Mr. Truth-Justice-and-the-American-Way and chat with him about how he is making the world safe for democracy. Kate reads my essays—all except this one—and occasionally inquires into my love life. They say women always know, but in this instance I suspect she doesn't. Last week's developments more or less assured me of her innocence:

We were at "our" café. Kate was telling me about her plans to visit a college roommate in Shreveport, plans sidetracked by the cost of a plane ticket.

"Shreveport," I said. "How about I drive you?"*

That earned me a caramel laugh and a flick of her hair.

"I have a close friend in Shreveport," I added. "It'll be fun."

So we bargained. We strategized. We divided the labor.

We made a plan to develop a more detailed plan.

The only problem is that I *don't* have a close friend in Shreveport. Quite frankly, I don't know a soul within two hundred miles of Shreveport. Until this week I wasn't sure whether Shreveport was in Arkansas or Louisiana.

That won't stop me, of course. I can already envision us sharing french fries at truck stops, stargazing along the Natchez Trace, asking campsite attendants to snap our photograph. What's fifteen hundred miles when the stakes are true love?

---

* I make foolish offers like this on occasion. Five years ago I drove a woman to New Orleans under similar circumstances.

I'll keep the "true love" part to myself, though. In the first place, I sense that Kate's not interested in romance. Not with me. Not now. And I am unprepared for rejection. It isn't love, requited or unrequited, that makes the world go round. It is hope.

Opting Out

I had been serving as God's assistant for three weeks when I first encountered Mrs. Y. She was an ancient Russian widow from a rural village, a woman who appeared as though she'd stepped off the pages of a Turgenev novel and into the medicine ward at the frenzied New York City hospital where she now lay confined to a gurney. She had likely been a great beauty once—you could still detect the scaffold of her delicate features beneath her withered skin—but her past splendor had proven no match for the aggressive cancer that had crept from her lungs into her bones. An angry bulb of tumor had already sprouted through the flesh behind her left shoulder. Resting atop a mound of pillows, her eyes closed, her face limned by carefully braided wisps of steel-gray hair, Mrs. Y appeared truly angelic, and if not for the shallow ebb and flow of her breath, one might have thought that she'd already assumed her rightful place in the celestial choir. Modern medicine had nothing left to offer Mrs. Y: no miracle drugs, no experimental procedures, no oncologic Houdinis to saw her in half and reassemble the parts. The grim, inescapable reality was that Mrs. Y was going to die. Everybody who had stepped foot inside Mrs. Y's hospital room over the preceding three days understood this—*except Mrs. Y.* Or if she did suspect her fate, which was certainly possible, then she had tapped into that macabre sixth sense we human beings possess for detecting our own impending mortality. What I knew for certain was that nobody on the medical staff had informed the patient of her diagnosis.

The reason that Mrs. Y remained unaware that she had only months—maybe weeks—to live was that her daughter, Mrs. A, had forbidden the doctors from telling her. I met with Mrs. A in an over-lit corridor opposite a bustling nurse's station. The daughter, a highly articulate and well-educated woman with a heavy Slavic accent, clearly was frazzled by her repeated clashes with my white-coated brethren, many of whom were half her age, but you sensed that she possessed both sound judgment and an abundance of heartfelt affection for her dying mother. "If you tell my mother she has cancer," explained Mrs. A, saying the "C" word tentatively, in a hushed voice, like my own mother's long-deceased spinster aunts, "You'll crush all of the hope and joy she has inside her. My mother is a Russian woman—she lived in Russia for seventy years—and *in Russia* we don't tell our loved-ones that they're going to die." Mrs. A explained that Mrs. Y's father had died of gastric cancer, many years earlier, and that Mrs. Y had been among the relatives who'd kept his condition a secret from both him and his wife. "My mother is suffering enough already. She understands that she's very sick. She wouldn't want to know any more than that." When I explained to Mrs. A that the senior medical resident had asked Mrs. Y point-blank that very morning whether she wanted to know the true nature of her illness, and that her mother had responded with an unequivocal yes, the daughter did not betray a glimmer of surprise. "Of course, she did," answered Mrs. A. "Because she assumed that it would be good news—and who wouldn't want good news? The idea that her own doctor might share bad news with her is inconceivable." I can only hope that, when *my* number comes due, I am privileged with as convincing and as passionate an advocate as Mrs. Y's daughter.

The reason for Mrs. A's conflict with her mother's doctors is that modern American medicine subscribes to a paradigm of full disclosure. In the United States—unlike in Russia—we *do* tell our elderly relatives that they are going to die. Our society has come to view knowing our medical prognosis as a fundamental right, and we uniformly expect our physicians to tell us *all*. It is worth noting that this has not always been the case. A pioneering study conducted by psychiatrist Donald Oken in 1961 revealed that, as recently as the Kennedy years, 88 percent of American physicians did *not* tell their patients of a cancer diagnosis. The broad spectrum of victims to this conspiracy of silence have included jazz bandleader Count Basie, the fictional tycoon "Big Daddy" in Tennessee Williams's *Cat on a Hot Tin Roof,* and my own maternal grandmother, who succumbed to breast cancer in 1955. Nor are Russians alone in their preference for nondisclosure. Physicians routinely withhold cancer diagnoses in much of East Asia, Africa, and the Middle East. When the Japanese emperor Hirohito died of duodenal carcinoma in 1987, he did so as doctors continued to reassure him that his cancer tests were negative. But Mrs. Y had not sought medical treatment in Tokyo. She'd entered a twenty-first-century American hospital—and now her family was requesting what might generously be termed a mid-twentieth-century approach to her care. That explained why I had been summoned, in my capacity as God's assistant, to offer a dose of Solomonic wisdom.

My official title, of course, was not "God's assistant." I was actually as far as one can possibly get from the divine and the omnipotent in this universe without asphyxiating on brimstone. Namely, I was a fourth-year medical student. But, for one month that winter, I had secured a position as an aide to the hospital's chief clinical ethicist, Dr. P, a world-renowned pulmonologist in his mid-sixties who doubled as chairman of the institution's ethics committee. Two decades earlier Dr. P had inherited a fledgling clinical ethics service, and, without any formal training in bioethics or philosophy, he had built it into one of the premier programs in the nation. His grandfatherly demeanor instilled confidence, and his rich baritone laugh was enough to disarm the most skeptical critic. Adding to Dr. P's authority were his religious convictions, as an Orthodox Jew, which he obviously drew on as a source of personal mooring. What made Dr. P most remarkable, however, was his abiding humility. Although he was called on multiple times each day to render advice on matters of life and death, he had not acquired the delusion of infallibility that all too often afflicts opinion leaders in both medicine and ethics. So when I described myself as laboring as God's assistant, which is how I explained my work to my friends and family, I did so in a spirit of irony—but also as a private, internally directed warning that I was *not* playing God, that my judgment, like Dr. P's, was merely one human being's highly skewed perspective. The truth was that I couldn't claim to be a run-of-the-mill fourth-year medical student. In my previous incarnation as an attorney, I had taught bioethics at the university level for nearly a decade before returning to professional school in my thirties—and I had published widely in the fields of healthcare law and end-of-life decision-making. I had all the more need to remind myself that whatever limited authority I did possess as an ethics consultant did not endow me with any monopoly on the truth. If there is a corporate hierarchy of moral insight, I suppose I was interning in God's mailroom.

I listened to both Mrs. A and to the senior medical resident without taking sides, mulling over the merits of their respective arguments, and then I reported back to Dr. P's office. The framework for discussing cases on the clinical ethics service involved gathering around the pulmonologist's enormous wooden desk with several of my colleagues—another fourth-year medical student, a third-year house officer—and hashing out our various perspectives on the dilemma at hand. Often these cases are intensely disturbing: Should the family of a carpenter whose arms and legs have been amputated as a result of a rare infection be permitted to withdraw further care from the patient, "believing that he wouldn't want to live as a helpless torso," without a written advance directive from the sick man? May a woman whose husband has suffered a burst aneurysm have the comatose man's sperm harvested before his life support is withdrawn so that she may conceive their child? These questions do not afford easy answers. The most challenging conundrums are forwarded to the hospital's standing committee on ethics, where specialists from various fields bring their professional judgment to bear on problems with no good answers, only necessary ones. But the case of Mrs. Y demanded rapid judgment. Her physicians had scheduled a family meeting for later that afternoon—and their intention was to inform the daughter that they had both a legal and a moral duty to tell Mrs. Y that she was dying. Only a firm directive from Dr. P and his helpers had the power to halt this process. But did the situation merit such an instruction? And how should we go about analyzing the dispute? That was what Dr. P wanted to know, leaning over his paper-shrouded desk, his gray eyebrows raised and his chin perched atop his thumb.

I distilled the case, as I saw it, to my colleagues: Mrs. A was invoking what I like to call the Frank Sinatra rule: "I'll Do It My Way"—or, since she was speaking for her mother, "We'll Do It Our Way." We might honor their wishes in the name of cultural difference, acknowledging that Russian notions of autonomy are different from our own. In contrast, the doctors preferred to follow what I call the Frank Loesser rule, after the lyricist who wrote "The Company Way" for the musical *How To Succeed in Business Without Really Trying*. According to Loesser, "the company"—in this case, the medical staff—had developed its policies for sound reasons. In short, "Doctor Knows Best." Although the details of Mrs. Y's case were distinctive, and memorable, the underlying conflict was one that arises daily while offering ethics advice to practicing physicians. Over and over again, we are forced to confront the same vexing question—the question on which Mrs. Y's fate depended: how far from societal norms do a person's wishes have to stand before we no longer afford that person the opportunity to opt out?

Jehovah's Witnesses believe that willfully accepting whole-blood transfusions, even during a medical emergency, will prevent the recipient from achieving eternal life after the Armageddon. They do not doubt the efficacy of these transfusions; the literature of their own governing body, the Watchtower organization, acknowledges that such interventions "may result in immediate . . . prolongation of life." However, Jehovah's Witnesses interpret chapter 15, verse 29, of the biblical book of Acts to mean that those sinners who accept this temporary lifesaving therapy may expose themselves to eternal damnation. As a professional bioethicist, I have very little authority to speak on the subject of eternal damnation—a matter about which scientific inquiry has yet to generate a consensus, one way or another. However, I have spent many years teaching and writing about the medical values of Jehovah's

Witnesses, as this religious minority offers a paradigmatic example of an established community that has chosen to opt out of mainstream medical practice. What is most striking about the refusal of Jehovah's Witnesses to accept blood is not that they die for their beliefs—although they do. It is that we let them do so.

One of the most precarious compromises of American medical ethics is that we allow competent, rational adults to refuse medical care—even when doing so will kill them. For example, in a highly publicized case in 2007, humorist Art Buchwald refused life-saving dialysis treatments, telling talk show host Diane Rehm that "If you have to go, the way you go is a big deal." The prospect of forcing such treatments on the octogenarian comic was never seriously discussed. At the same time, our society adopts an entirely different standard with regard to children belonging to communities that attempt to opt out of our societal norms. In such cases, we do *not* defer to the individual's or family's requests. So while physicians will let a nineteen-year-old Jehovah's Witness bleed to death on the operating table, sooner than contravene the patient's express desires, a seventeen-year-old who avows similar beliefs will be forcibly transfused. To the Witness congregation, of course, the distinction is utterly meaningless. Damnation doesn't wait for the age of majority. Yet this birth-date-based distinction between the right to opt out and "the company way" is the mode that we have adopted to balance two fundamentally incompatible worldviews. We apply this same standard to Christian Scientists who refuse antibiotics and to Scientologists who reject psychiatry. As Wiley Rutledge, a Massachusetts Supreme Court justice, wrote in the seminal case of *Prince vs. Massachusetts,* "Parents may be free to become martyrs themselves. But it does not follow they are free, in identical circumstances, to make martyrs of their children before they have reached the age . . . when they can make that choice for themselves." If our legal tradition has less to say about making martyrs of our elderly parents, like Mrs. Y, this may be because, until recently, few of us had the "good fortune" to survive into our golden years.

Whether or not we accept Justice Rutledge's approach as the most reasonable one, we must recognize that these competing value systems can be balanced in other ways. A second school of legal thought—albeit one that has gained far less traction in the American bioethics community—rejects the distinction between children and adults in favor of one that distinguishes between "internal" and "external" conduct. Justice Robert Jackson, Rutledge's nemesis on the court on issues of religion, explained this approach as follows: "I think the limits [on individual autonomy] begin to operate whenever activities begin to affect or collide with liberties of others or the public. Religious activities which concern only members of the faith are and ought to be free—as nearly absolutely free as anything can be." However, according to Jackson, once a religious minority's behavior affects individuals outside their own community, then it becomes one of "Caesar's affairs" and society has every right to intervene. So the Jacksonian model would permit Witness children to reject transfusions, even if the result was that they hemorrhaged themselves straight into immortality. However, this same model would not let the off-spring of Christian Scientists refuse childhood vaccinations, because doing so creates a disease reservoir that can imperil the health of children not affiliated with the sect. Although Rutledge's rubric is the framework most frequently used in medicine today, there are areas outside the field of health care where our society follows Jackson's reasoning and does allow insular religious and cultural communities to opt their children out of widely held societal norms. For example, many states permit Amish teenagers to learn agriculture and woodworking at home, rather than the algebra and civics curricula otherwise mandated by education guidelines, because these adolescents grow up to become self-sufficient farmers and craftsmen whose decision to opt out has only a minimal impact on the general welfare.

The problem with the approaches of both Justice Rutledge and Justice Jackson is that there is some consensual conduct that, even when confined to adults and relegated to the bounds of a self-sufficient community, most Americans refuse to tolerate. A physician in the United States who performs a "circumcision" on an eighteen-year-old Somali girl will lose his license to practice medicine and may be sent to prison—even if the patient actively sought the controversial procedure, which is widely condoned in the Horn of Africa. Much as our society refuses to tolerate adult incest or polygamy, regardless of whether the participants themselves embrace the behavior, we often draw a line at certain medical and medically related interventions that, quite frankly, make us queasy: self-castration, trepanation, elective limb amputation. If your culture embraces endocannibalism—the consumption of human corpses, often as a sign of reverence for the departed—as do the Mayora people of Peru and the Fore tribe of Papua—you are not welcome to opt out of our norms. I do not mean either to endorse or to criticize these limits on personal and cultural autonomy. My only intention is to make clear that, all theoretical frameworks and bioethical paradigms aside, there do exist certain practices that our society will not permit simply because these practices stray too far from our own cultural mores.

Decisions relating to death and dying are among those about which our society is least likely to allow dissident individuals and cultural minorities to opt out. We may permit competent adults to turn down heroic, life-prolonging medical care—but that is as far as our indulgence extends. A particularly enlightening example of what we do *not* tolerate is revealed in the passing of Admiral Chester Nimitz Jr., the son of the celebrated Pacific Fleet commander. When the 86-year-old Nimitz and his 89-year-old wife, Joan, committed suicide together in 2002, both were ailing, but neither spouse was terminally ill. Yet, as the naval hero wrote in his final note, "Our decision was made over a considerable period of time and was not carried out in acute desperation. Nor is it the expression of a mental illness. We have consciously, rationally, deliberately and of our own free will taken measures to end our lives today because of the physical limitations on our quality of life placed upon us by age, failing vision, osteoporosis, back and painful orthopedic problems." Not even the states of Oregon, Washington, and Montana—which allow assisted suicide for the dying under tightly subscribed circumstances—would have permitted the Nimitzes to opt out in this extreme manner. In fact any health-care provider who assisted the couple in ending their lives would have faced common-law prosecution in their home state of Massachusetts. Fortunately I was not called on to effectuate the end-of-life wishes of Admiral Nimitz. All I had to determine was whether Mrs. Y should be told that she had cancer, which seems like a much smaller pot of hemlock to swallow. Or is it? Because once we allow some people to start dying "their own way"—let's say by refusing to learn the full extent of their illnesses—how will we ever be able to tell others that they have to die "our" way? As every law student learns at the outset of training: "Hard cases make bad law."

I approach the question of "opt out" from an unusual perspective, as I am both a member of the medical establishment and, in my personal preferences, a staunch dissenter from its norms. I have always harbored suspicions regarding our cultural emphasis on the prolongation of life, at nearly any cost, but my views ultimately crystallized over the course of my grandfather's final illness. A robust, hardy man into his mid-eighties, Grandpa Leo fell ill one night while enjoying a home-cooked dinner of chicken cutlets. I was seated between him and my grandmother, in the same linoleum-padded kitchen where I'd once scampered as a toddler, when his precise jeweler's hands started shaking with violence, and his dinner fork clanked furiously against his plate. The next few minutes, en route to the nearest emergency room, marked the last time that my grandfather displayed full control of his body or a meaningful grasp of his circumstances. Then something went haywire. A stroke? An electrolyte imbalance that melted his gray matter? The cause of his sudden cognitive and physical decline will remain one of science's unsolved mysteries—in part because, shortly after his hospitalization, all efforts to solve it ceased. What mattered was that his state was irreversible. *That,* and only *that,* his physicians could all agree on. And so began our family's thirteen-month descent through the inner circles of hell.

While money was a concern, we pretended that it wasn't. I suppose Grandpa Leo, who came of age impoverished in Depression-era Belgium, would have been aghast to discover how much we paid the mercenary Haitian nurse's aide to sponge his skin and change his diapers during my grandfather's first days back at home. Our newfound helper was a broad-grinned man in his twenties with a sharp, satanic beard—and if the Jehovah's Witnesses are correct about the Apocalypse, I am confident he will be boiled eternally in the same cauldron with those who take extra servings of blood. Never have I seen a man treat a fellow human being so roughly, heaving my grandfather from bed to chair like a sack of spoiled sugar. I believe this arrangement lasted approximately forty-eight hours. Then came the "deluxe" nursing home, where a caged blue-and-gold macaw squawked for her freedom in the lobby. The patients kept largely to their own rooms, as though embarrassed to be seen in their states of cascading decay. Yet the flower displays changed daily, baroque fugues of dahlias and tiger lilies. The walnut furniture was immaculately polished—like the interior of a coffin. One sensed from the decor that the owners were merely waiting for the residents to die off so that they could open an investment bank.

Two months later, when the insurers finally had their say, Grandpa Leo was demoted to a human warehouse beside a shuttered community hospital. Here the nurses were plump, friendly creatures, and the demented and disfigured inmates gathered in the corridors to display their woes without shame. Visits proved quite tolerable, really, if one could endure the home's mild yet pervasive stench of urine.

I will forgo a detailed description of the intermittent hospital visits—of which, as when dealing with most incapacitated senior citizens, there were many: mild heart attacks, aspiration pneumonias, sepsis. When my grandfather finally died, he had not uttered a single word in a month or opened his eyes in more than two weeks. He required a ventilator to conduct his breathing, a hole in his stomach to supply his nutrition, multiple lines to infuse his veins with antibiotics and fluids and morphine. I was told that his entire backside, from his neck to his ankles, had bruised the color of a ripe plum—although I did not have the courage to look. My grandfather had always said, "Where there is life, there is hope," which may explain—

at least, in part—our family's reluctance to withdraw care. But the unfortunate reality is that, where there is life, there is often false hope too.

Fortunately I come from a family of physicians. My father and my uncle, with sixty years of doctoring between them, had the wisdom to cry uncle before Grandpa Leo's medical team called in the heavy artillery: dialysis to replace my grandfather's failed kidneys, vasoconstrictors to keep his blood pressure from bottoming out, electrode pads to shock his heart into action every time the organ took a well-earned rest. That is death in the postmodern age. The noblest of professions has managed to create machines of torture more potent than the cruelest devices of the Inquisition.

That is not how my grandfather wanted to die. And it is not how I want to die.

I am fully aware of all the technological wonders that modern medicine has to offer. However, when I reach the point where I can no longer enjoy lucid, fulfilling conversations with my loved ones, my personal preference would be for the medical staff to place a plastic bag over my head during my sleep. I do not want to live life in a wheelchair or with a missing limb or even dependent on an aide to do my shopping. If the likelihood of my making a complete physical and mental recovery from whatever ailment or injury befalls me should ever dip below about 80 percent, I would sooner perish on the spot than risk a possible future of permanent debilitation. Needless to say, I recognize that many people live meaningful lives with missing limbs and cognitive impairments. Floyd Skloot, possibly the most gifted essayist of our time, writes through the fog of a brain-liquefying virus that punched holes in his gray matter at the age of forty-one. Stephen Hawking, unable to feed himself, is unraveling the mysteries of the universe. Jean-Dominique Bauby, the paralyzed French journalist, blinked his memoir, *The Diving Bell and the Butterfly*, with the use of one eyelid. So I readily acknowledge that one can lead a meaningful life while suffering from such a disability, and I do not wish to diminish the contributions of those fearless souls who do so. However, I am determined never to be one of them. All the power to them for savoring their pleasures, but that is not the variety of life *I* am willing to lead.

Whatever else you may think of my preferences—and even Dr. P, a man who has witnessed the full gamut of the human condition, finds them utterly befuddling—rest assured that they are not the half-cocked ideas of the uninformed. I have spent years studying the literature of death and disability, teaching students about autonomy and beneficence, advising patients and legal clients on the intricacies of writing living wills. Quite frankly I suspect there are few individuals in the entire country who have devoted as many hours as I have to reflecting on how I want to die. I can safely say that I am the only person I know who carries my advance directive around with me in my wallet, between my driver's license and my credit cards: the *only* person—and many of my friends are professional bioethicists! So I know my own heart. I also recognize that, in wishing for the senior house officer to place a plastic bag over my head when I can no longer complete a *New*

York Times crossword puzzle, my preferences deviate considerably further from the norm than those of Mrs. Y's daughter. I suppose that if Mrs. A ever learned my own thoughts on "opting out" of medical care, she might fear I was crazy. Even in Russia, the senior house officers won't place a plastic bag over your head. Of course, Mrs. A will not have an opportunity to talk me out of opting out. One of the strangest ironies of our fast-paced and impersonal medical world is that while I know all about Mrs. A's wishes, she will never know anything of mine.

Mrs. Y's doctors had scheduled their meeting with her family for three P.M. The digital clock behind Dr. P's desk read 2:47. Then Dr. P's phone rang, and he spoke for several minutes with a man whose wife was dying of emphysema—a reminder of the pulmonologist's other weighty responsibilities. While we waited for our leader, my colleagues passed the time chatting about residency interviews and the prospects for a national electronic medical records system. They did not mention Mrs. Y, as though doing so without Dr. P would violate some unspoken rule of decorum, much like sequestered jurors who do not continue their deliberations over lunch. When Dr. P did turn to me again, apologizing for the interruption and seeking my wisdom regarding Mrs. Y, the clock read 2:56.

While Dr. P had been on the phone and my colleagues had been discussing the merits and dangers of automated charts, I had been thinking about Mrs. A and how painful it must be to sit beside her dying mother, morning and afternoon, while pretending that all would turn out well. I recollected the toll of my own grandmother's daily visits to Grandpa Leo. The reality was that, as the old judicial adage tells us, deciding Mrs. Y's case justly was easy—but explaining that decision required the wisdom of a talented jurist.

"We shouldn't tell her," I announced decisively. "While full disclosure is an important value that cannot be dismissed lightly, this is a classic case of therapeutic privilege."

Therapeutic privilege is an obscure doctrine in bioethics that permits withholding a diagnosis in cases where providing certain information to the patient would likely reduce her chances of survival. The principle permits physicians to carve out an exception to our society's strong preference for full disclosure, so it is invoked very rarely. Academic bioethicists write about the concept with great gusto in theoretical treatises, but the truth of the matter was that, in my entire time in clinical ethics, I had never before witnessed another physician or ethicist apply it in practice. Nor, to be completely candid, have I ever seen anybody invoke it since. But from 2:56 to 2:58 that afternoon, I made a compelling case that telling Mrs. Y of her cancer would significantly damage her health.

My most powerful ammunition came from the tail end of the conversation that I'd had with Mrs. A, once I had decided that I would do my utmost to assist her. I'd learned in law school, many years earlier, that changing the law was never as easy as shifting the facts, so I had pressed the daughter to tell me more about her grandfather's death. "Did your mother keep his cancer a secret because she feared it might make his condition worse? That it might take away his will to recover?" I asked.

"Yes," answered Mrs. A. "Exactly."

"And did your mother ever say that, if *she* were dying of cancer, she wouldn't want to know because the diagnosis would take away *her own* will to recover?"

Mrs. A frowned doubtfully. "Why are you asking me this?"

"I am trying to help you," I explained. "If your mother previously told you that if she knew she had cancer, she would give up on life, I can make a stronger argument to the senior doctors that we should not reveal her diagnosis to her." I considered patting Mrs. A's stiff shoulder to break the wall of suspicion between us but thought the better of it. "Now think carefully. Did your mother ever say that, if *she* were dying of cancer, knowing that she had cancer would break her will?"

Mrs. A nodded vigorously. "Exactly. She said it would crush her."

I have no way of knowing for certain whether Mrs. Y's daughter was telling me the truth about recalling this conversation or even if she actually had a grandfather who had died of gastric cancer. Many of my colleagues might have pushed Mrs. A further on the matter—asking for the details of these conversations or demanding the corroboration of witnesses. I cannot imagine why. I went to medical school to help people, after all, not to cross-examine them. If Mrs. A was willing to tell me that these words had been exchanged, I'd gladly accept them as facts—even if it had required a dose of helpful contextualization to jog the poor woman's memory. So I pitched the case for nondisclosure to my fellow ethics consultants, emphasizing Mrs. Y's own alleged wishes.

"I've heard enough," declared Dr. P. "You were smart to ask about Mrs. Y's father."

The wall clock read exactly 3:00—just as it might in an impeccably plotted adventure film. Dr. P handed me his telephone, and I called Mrs. Y's physician. To my surprise, when I told him that we saw no need for full-disclosure, he responded, "I'm glad. We didn't want to tell her, you know, but we didn't think we had any choice in the matter."

I do not know when or how Mrs. Y died. I had done my part—and I left it to others to palliate her pain and attend to her final wants. But her angelic face remains printed indelibly in my memory, a reminder of how much, in our final days, we are all dependent on the mercies of others. We live in a world where well-meaning strangers in white coats will determine under what circumstances, and to what extent, we can opt out of their standards. I only hope that, if I'm ever lying helpless on a gurney, no longer able to shape my own destiny, someone cares enough to nudge the facts in my favor.

Charming and Devoted

I had braced myself for medical Armageddon—for hundreds of disease-ravaged bodies in simultaneous death throes—but my first two patients are actually in better shape than I am. Both men are mildly senile, saddled with benign bladder ailments.* Of the 216 years we share among us, I have contributed only 36, while Mr. C. and Mr. D. have both eclipsed the nine-decade mark. Somehow, despite this age disparity, I am supposed to be dishing out wisdom. I am the doctor, after all—even if I have been on the wards for less than one week. The only professional insight I have to offer so far is that being a pleasantly forgetful nonagenarian seems far less stressful than serving as a medical intern at a major New York City hospital.

*Several minor personal details in this essay have been intentionally altered to protect the medical confidentiality of the depicted patients and their survivors.

Such is the demographic paradox of a junior physician's relationship with his patients: I worry about how to extend their lives. This anxiety inevitably shortens my own.

Mr. C.—whom I will hereafter call Mr. Charming, although the "C" actually stands for a hyphenated Puerto Rican surname—may be the healthiest patient in the entire medical center. When I meet him, approximately twelve hours after he wanders into the emergency room complaining of pain upon urination, he has already traded in his hospital gown for a guayabera shirt and a stylish panama hat. If he were to tell me that he'd once starred in silent films alongside Ramón Novarro, I'd believe him, although it turns out that he actually served as a chauffeur for several prominent Chasidic rabbis. Mr. Charming readily admits that he forgets "small things": the day of the week, whether or not he has injected his mealtime insulin. He "wings" it. "So far," he assures me, "so good." While his memory may be fading, his sense of humor remains intact. I ask him why he has come to our hospital, while in the past he has sought care elsewhere. "Your nurses are prettier than theirs," he says, matter-of-fact. Then he grins broadly.

Mr. D.—short for "Devoted," and also for a longer German-Jewish name—has come to the hospital by ambulance with Mrs. D., a retired nurse, who hardly ever leaves his bedside during visiting hours. "We've been married for sixty-three years," she explains. Her husband, a gentle-featured man with big, innocent eyes bulging under heavy lids, adds, "married *to each other*," and at the moment I'm not sure whether he's clarifying or joking. Soon I will realize that he cannot possibly be joking, because Mr. Devoted is as earnest as he is loyal. Every evening, he awakens from his postprandial nap, alarmed for the welfare of his wife. "What if she's sick?" he asks. "What if she needs a doctor?" She is *not* sick, I explain. She does *not* need a doctor. Mrs. Devoted will return in the morning. "Oh, that's good," he agrees, his relief instantaneous. "I was afraid that she was sick, but I couldn't remember her name."

The hospital can do little for Mr. Devoted's dementia, but we've already cured his hydronephrosis—a condition in which the bladder clogs and urine backs up into the kidneys. It's nothing that a well-placed Foley catheter can't cure. Other doctors have already inserted this tube into his urethra in the emergency room, and by the time I examine Mr. Devoted twenty-four hours later, he's feeling "ready to go home." I've been awake since four o'clock in the morning, and it's now late afternoon, so I tell him the truth: "So am I."

The plan is for both Mr. Charming and Mr. Devoted to depart in a few days, as soon as the former's antibiotics kick in and the latter's kidney function returns to normal. In the interim they have been assigned to the same room—in the western wing of the hospital, overlooking a courtyard designed by architect I. M. Pei—a quirk of administrative fate that will prove unspeakably convenient for me while making my pre-dawn rounds.

As I prepare to sign my pager over to the night team, I poke my head into their room to make sure that my two patients are comfortable.

"Do you need anything before I leave?"

Mr. Devoted leans forward on his elbows, his pale forearms tinged purple beneath the fluorescent light. "Tell my wife that I'm here," he requests.

I promise him that I will.

I turn to his roommate. "How about you, Mr. C.? Can I get you anything?"

"What I want," he answers, "you can't give me."

"I'm not sure I understand. What is it that you want?"

Mr. Charming moves his hands through the air. For a split second, I think that he is trying to pantomime a medical need—and then I realize that his fingers are tracing the hourglass shape of a well-curved female. His dumb-show complete, Mr. Charming smiles sheepishly, like a wayward child.

"Hang in there," I urge him.

"I'm an old man, but I'm not so old. I don't feel like an old man, doctor," says Mr. Charming. "You see what I'm saying?"

I *do* see what he is saying. And I am entirely unable to help.

Mr. Charming's antibiotics work their magic, but he will not return home. That is the decision of my boss, the senior attending, who has concluded that our would-be lothario doesn't think lucidly enough to survive on his own. At stake is not just buying groceries or paying bills, but those pesky mealtime insulin shots that forestall hyperglycemic comas and rapid death. In that sense Mr. Charming is much like tens of thousands of other mildly impaired elderly men and women who stumble into the health-care system each year, usually as a result of relatively minor ailments, but are deemed unfit to stumble back out. I long ago concluded that these patients *should* be permitted to return home, if they so choose—that the risks of a diabetic coma or a terminal hip fracture may be far preferable to an extra six months of a life spent trapped inside a nursing home. In this age of advanced technology, a narrow chasm separates health care from torture. Imprisoning elderly patients for their own good is one way in which doctors plunge into this abyss, and I am determined never to do so. Realistically such decisions still remain well above my pay grade.

If Mr. Charming wished to leave, I would embrace his cause—advocating up the chain of command to the hospital's chief medical officer, if necessary. Fortunately my patient has decided that he *enjoys* being in the hospital: the prepared food, the companionship of Mr. Devoted, the attractive nurses. "I like my new home very much," he tells me, when I examine him several days later. Someone has even brought many of his personal effects to the hospital, and a vintage three-piece suit now hangs in his closet. He is Medicare's worst nightmare: a hale and vigorous senior citizen, living for free in a hospital room at the cost of roughly $1,000 each night.

I discuss Mr. Charming's future with his social worker. She has become rather enchanted with the patient, who apparently still displays a way with the ladies—although he leaves an avuncular, rather than romantic, impression. If he occasionally tells me off-color jokes about pregnant prostitutes, his conduct with the ward's female staff is impeccable. Lucy, who declares, "I just adore that man," has spent considerable energy on his case. Alas she has made absolutely no progress. It turns out that Mr. Charming is thoroughly alone in the world. He hasn't spoken to his "no good" son in forty-four years, his only niece has disconnected her telephone, and his many friends, he informs me apologetically, "are all dead." This would not be a problem, except that Medicare, which will pay for one hundred days of hospital treatment, will not shell out a dime for a nursing home. Mr. Charming actually has private insurance too, but Lucy informs me that his is a "crummy" plan. I have since discovered that all patients have coverage plans that vary between "crummy" and "lousy," including the insurance provided by the hospital to its junior physicians. The best health-care wisdom one acquires as a medical intern is alarmingly simple: never get sick.

Most patients who must relocate to a nursing facility rely on Medicaid, which funds long-term care for individuals who cannot afford it themselves. Unfortunately Mr. Charming *can* afford it. He apparently has quite a small fortune stashed away, which he intends to spend on his next girlfriend. "A man's got to have money for the women," he explains. Nothing short of a court order can force him to part with these funds, and establishing financial guardianship—if his case does eventually require that—might take months. Moreover, once his Medicare runs out, the hospital cannot ethically evict him. Instead the institution will likely swallow the costs of his stay, however long that may be. In short Mr. Charming has unwittingly found a loophole that might allow him to live out his remaining days eating sugar-free pancakes in plastic containers and flirting with busty physical therapists.

I'm pondering Mr. Charming's dilemma, and now juggling a caseload of several other, much sicker patients, when I'm paged by the nurse taking care of Mr. Devoted. The old man wishes to speak with me immediately. With some patients, *all* requests are urgent, but Mr. Devoted has never been one to cry wolf. The truth is that he rarely asks for anything other than reassurance that his wife is well. I politely excuse myself from my midday conference—a mandatory lecture on "risk management" to which all junior house officers are subjected—and race westward.

I find Mr. Devoted with his face in his hands, his long white hair ghostlike on his pale shoulders. His wife is not with him this morning. She has been held up by a freak overnight squall that has toppled trees onto parked cars throughout Manhattan. I gently touch Mr. Devoted's elbow. He looks up, startled.

"I have troubles, doctor," he says. "Real troubles."

"Anything I can help you with?"

Mr. Devoted groans. He glances around the room—taking in his own spare, sterile alcove and the cluttered, homey section where Mr. Charming is now dozing. Then he leans toward me, his voice lowered to a whisper, and he confesses, "I can't afford any of this."

He catches me off-guard. I had expected a physiological complaint.

"This must cost an awful lot of money, doctor," he continues. "I'm not sure who told you that I can pay for this, but I can't. I don't have any money at all."

I pat his frail shoulder to console him. "This is all free. Medicare is paying for this. All you have to do is get better. That's your only responsibility right now."

He eyes me suspiciously. "Free?"

"Free for you," I emphasize. "You have nothing to worry about."

"I don't want to leave my wife with nothing," he says. "We're poor people, but a woman has to have something to live on."

I sense Mr. Charming's influence here, but it's hard to imagine the Puerto Rican ladies' man offering financial advice. More likely Mr. Devoted has picked up threads of my conversation with his roommate and woven them into a tapestry of his own.

"I'll get you the money somehow," Mr. Devoted assures me. "I'll go to the man in charge, and I'll tell him I need it."

I suppose the "man in charge" is a one-time employer, a boss from my patient's days as a textile worker. It would be relieving to know that there was a "man in charge" at present too—of the hospital, of the cosmos—someone or something attempting to order the chaos of life on the wards. I am doubtful.

"You don't need to pay me right now," I assure Mr. Devoted. "Once you get better, *then* we can talk about the bill."

Mr. Devoted smiles. This arrangement seems far more plausible to him than the prospect of free care.

"That sounds very reasonable," he says. "Thank you, doctor."

"You're going home tomorrow," I tell him. "We're going to send you home with the Foley catheter in place."

"If you say so," he agrees. "Will you tell my wife?"

"She already knows."

"That's good," he says. "I don't want her to think I'm missing."

Mr. Devoted's departure plans are short-lived.

I am working late that night. I've had an argument with the hospital's billing office earlier that afternoon because I dared submit a written discharge summary for one of my patients. This particular summary, a description of the patient's hospital course provided to third-party insurers for reimbursement purposes, is apparently supposed to be dictated into a voice recorder. A printed document will not suffice. So I am reading my discharge summary into the telephone, knowing that this recording will then be shipped to Bangalore, where a cash-strapped Indian college student will convert my words back into text, likely laced with a smattering of typographical errors and creative spellings, when I receive word that Mr. Devoted is bleeding profusely. I hang up on my South Asian scribe, midsentence, and jog the darkened corridors of the hospital. Running in a long, white coat proves a challenge. My stethoscope gets caught on a doorknob and loses an earpiece.

When I finally arrive at Mr. Devoted's room, the overnight team is already managing his care. Mr. Charming leans against a nearby wall, a debonair spectator in bathrobe and slippers, sipping a contraband Coke.

The nature of the tragedy is rather straightforward: Mr. Devoted has tugged on his urinary catheter in a moment of confusion, lodging the inflated balloon in his distal urethra. Needless to say, the result is as painful as it is bloody: the human penis was never designed to disgorge an implement the size of a golf ball. Fortunately, the incident occurred inside the hospital, where skilled nurses have been able to remove the tube quickly and to staunch the resulting wound. However, this is not the end of the patient's misery, but the beginning. Now Mr. Devoted cannot be trusted to leave the catheter in place. He cannot return home unsupervised. He cannot be left alone. In the absence of continuous visual observation— a commodity that the hospital doles out even more reluctantly than free care—Mr. Devoted will have to wear specially designed mittens that will prevent him from hurting himself. They also keep him from doing much of anything else, from dialing a telephone to opening a milk carton. He has become a grown man with the dexterity of a declawed cat.

I explain the situation to Mrs. Devoted the following morning. By now her husband has already demonstrated an uncanny ability to extricate himself from the security mittens —he has actually gnawed his way through a portion of the mesh—and he is strapped to the bed with Posey restraints. Mrs. Devoted does not appear to be particularly concerned.

"We've been through so much already," she says.

"Mr. D. and I had a nice chat last night," I tell her—which is true. "He kept asking for you."

"Frankly, I'm surprised," she replies. "He usually doesn't remember my name."

"He remembered it last night," I assure her—although this is patently false.

As soon as the words leave my mouth, I realize that *I* do not know Mrs. Devoted's first name. If she were to ask me, my web of falsehood would quickly unravel. But I can sense from her dubious expression that she will not ask, because she already knows that I'm lying.

"Any word from the podiatrist?" she asks.

This is the fourth straight day that Mrs. Devoted has requested a visit from a foot specialist. She's fixated on her husband's toenails, which are slightly overgrown, and every afternoon I phone in a request for a podiatry consult that never arrives. It is an epic, existential battle. Now that Mr. Devoted has lost control of his hands, the welfare of his feet looms all the larger.

I understand Mrs. Devoted's fixation. Unclipped toenails are something that she *can* control, a problem capable of resolution. When my own grandfather fell terminally ill, my grandmother became overly concerned with the care of his false teeth. I cannot imagine what it is like to sit beside a man you've loved for nearly seven decades who can no longer remember your name.

"I wish I could arrange for an aide to sit with your husband," I explain to Mrs. Devoted. "I'll keep trying, but I can't make any promises."

The reality is that I've already tried. While the hospital will grudgingly furnish a "one-to-one" observer if you're suicidal—as they did for an Orthodox Jewish patient who wished to visit the chapel after an overdose attempt—obtaining such care for an elderly patient who is merely confused is nigh impossible. As the nurse manager in charge of staffing explained to me: "I'd have to rework the schedule for the entire floor, and I can't do that. What's wrong with keeping the man in restraints? He doesn't seem to mind, does he?" So my optimism in the presence of Mrs. Devoted is tempered by the knowledge that her husband would have to be a modern-day Houdini to escape his fetters.

I promise Mrs. Devoted that I'll sit with her husband as often as possible, so that he can have at least a brief respite from his ropes.

"You do that, doctor. Please do," she says. "And I tell you what I'm going to do. I'm going to call the podiatrist myself."

Meanwhile Mr. Charming is no longer my patient. As he suffers from no active medical condition, he has been transferred from my care to that of a nurse-practitioner. I will still greet him every morning on the way to examining Mr. Devoted, but I will no longer have to go through the motions of listening to his healthy heart or palpating his painless abdomen. At first this prospect is a relief. It means one less responsibility at six o'clock in the morning. But I am also nervous that the nurse-practitioner will review my prior notes on Mr. Charming, into which, as an outlet for my subversive instincts, I have been inserting apropos quotations from my lunchtime reading, *The Collected Short Stories of John Cheever.* If the hospital is ever sued by Mr. Charming's estate, I will have to explain the excessive references to suburbia and gin-based drinks. But I suspect that my successor fears asking about these strange interludes, maybe because she is hesitant to expose what she takes for gaps in her own knowledge. In any case days pass, and I hear no complaints about my aberrant conduct.

I am too busy to discuss this transfer of care with Mr. Charming, assuming that his new provider will explain the change. I shake his hand each morning, reserving my stethoscope for his roommate's lungs and stomach. Three days pass before he calls me on my act of desertion.

"Why aren't you my doctor anymore?" demands Mr. Charming.

"Because you're all better," I explain. "You're not sick anymore."

"Okay, I'm not sick anymore," agrees Mr. Charming. "But I still need a doctor."

Mr. Charming and Mr. Devoted have been in the hospital for three weeks. Mr. Devoted has been tied to his bed for the last five days. I am saddled with other patients—the critically ill victims of heart failure and cancer whom I'd anticipated at the outset. Several have died. I finally connect with the warning I received from a veteran physician prior to the start of my internship: "Soon enough, the patients will start to seem like your enemies." At the time I dismissed his comment as jaded hyperbole. Yet moments spent discussing minor concerns with my patients increasingly seem a distraction from the endless series of admission notes and follow-up orders that dominate my fifteen-hour days. I have not yet wanted one of my patients to die in order to decrease my workload. That is a line I hope that I never cross. But I confess that on several occasions I've wished that certain cantankerous patients, not suffering from life-threatening conditions, would check out of the hospital overnight against medical advice. Hippocrates might be disappointed, but Hippocrates never worked a ninety-hour week.

I am on my way to write a death certificate one morning, following a long overnight shift, when Mr. Charming flags me down in the corridor. My first instinct is to tell him that I can't help him at the moment—that he's no longer my patient, that I have another pressing responsibility—but then it hits me that my priorities are backwards if a death certificate takes precedence over a living patient.

"Sorry to disturb you, doctor," he says, "but Mr. D. is tied to the bed."

"I know," I explain. "That's for his safety. So he doesn't pull out the catheter."

"Okay, but his breakfast is here. How is he supposed to eat like that?"

The practicalities of Mr. Devoted's dining regimen had never crossed my mind. I have taken it for granted that one of the nurse's aides will assist him—and that morning, apparently a result of a staffing shortage, nobody has been assigned to his room.

"I know you're busy, doctor," presses Mr. Charming. "But the man has to eat."

"Of course he does," I agree. "I'll take care of it."

I foray into Mr. Devoted's room and promise him that I'll find someone to help him. He responds by wiggling his fingertips and shrugging.

Several nurses explain to me that helping patients eat is not a nursing duty, but a lower-order task assigned to one of the young aides sporting bright blue smocks. Usually these young women are ubiquitous. This morning none are to be found. I squander twenty minutes trying to convince various staff members to feed Mr. Devoted before I pawn off the duty for locating an aide onto the floor's business administrator. "It will be taken care of," I am told. Passive voice. I can already envision what will really happen: either Mr. Devoted will go without breakfast, or I will end up feeding him myself.

Onward! I navigate the back corridors of the hospital until I find the Dickensian chamber where death is transformed from a biological to a clerical phenomenon. The women who run this office are impressively relentless. They have been known for their efforts to summon physicians out of emergency procedures in order to complete paperwork for the medical examiner. I endure stoically as one of these overseers lectures me at length on the importance of "accuracy and precision" in describing the cause of death on the certificate, and I can't help wondering how she'd react if I attributed this patient's demise to "The Hand of God." Even as I type "cardiac arrest secondary to sepsis" on the form, I am contemplating an addendum that reads, "The Archangels Michael and Gabriel descended to earth and gathered the departed during her slumber." When I've completed my bureaucratic duties, I make a point of telling the overseer how grateful the departed would have been for her efforts. She thanks me politely, and I fear that my sarcasm has been lost on her.

On the western ward, as I've expected, no nurse's aide has arrived to assist Mr. Devoted. However, my services will not be needed. I peek into his room, and, to my amazement, there is Mr. Charming, sitting alongside Mr. Devoted's bed, feeding spoonfuls of breakfast cereal to his bound companion. I stand silently behind the curtain, watching as Mr. Charming holds up a juice carton and Mr. Devoted sips through a narrow straw, mesmerized by the simplicity of this kindness.

The following morning the verdict arrives that Mr. Devoted will be transferred to a nursing home. Like many decisions in the health-care system, this arrangement does not reflect a change of facts—the patient is no healthier, no less likely to pull out his catheter. Instead a new senior physician has come on duty and decided that Mr. Devoted may have his bladder emptied with a different type of temporary catheter at specific times of the day. I have argued for this solution for nearly a week, insisting to the senior resident that, had Mr. Devoted been his own father, he never would have tolerated such draconian measures. Up until the arrival of the new attending, however, inertia favored bondage. Now inertia favors freedom. The alternative is confining Mr. Devoted on the western ward indefinitely, until his bladder heals, which is not a realistic plan. "This is a hospital, not a hotel," the attending physician reminds me. I discuss the matter with Mrs. Devoted, and she agrees with this discharge plan. "The podiatrist has already seen him," she informs me. "What else can we do?"

I put off telling Mr. Devoted. I'm not sure that he will register the meaning of my words or that he will even care one way or the other, and I'd like him to savor his new liberty for a few hours before I burden him with any additional worries. I'm also reluctant to share the news in front of Mr. Charming. I cannot say whether these two men are actually friends—whether this is the sort of "lifelong" connection forged in mutual adversity or merely a transient intimacy, such as one makes with fellow passengers on an airplane or cruise ship. What does it even mean to make a new friend at ninety, when you're confined to a hospital and mildly demented? Yet as I ask myself this question, I already know the answer. It means *everything*. What renders us human is the ability to bond, to love, to feel loss, long after all our other faculties have evaporated. We are desperately social animals, even in twilight. As an agent of the American health-care system—"the best system in the world," I have been told—I am about to sever the most important relationship in Mr. Charming's life.

I find Mr. Charming in the lounge, sipping another illicit Coke. He's resting both of his hands on the head of his cane, while seated, like an Iberian field marshal posing for a portrait.

"Mr. D. will be leaving," I tell him. "We've found him a nursing home."

I am confident that revealing this information violates numerous federal confidentiality statutes.

Mr. Charming sighs. He looks vulnerable and naked without his trademark grin.

"A man has to go places," he says. "There's no stopping him."

I pat his knobby knee. "I thought you'd want to know."

"Who knows what a man wants to know?" he asks—addressing himself more than me. "You do what you think is best, doctor. That's all we ask of you."

I have been told that it will take several more days to place Mr. Devoted in a nursing home, because few facilities are interested in a patient who requires frequent catheterization, so I do not say good-bye that morning. The remainder of the afternoon is time off for me—a needed opportunity to sleep after a twenty-eight-hour shift. So when I return to the hospital the following morning, at six A.M., I feel well rested and rejuvenated for the first time in weeks.

I start my predawn rounds on the western ward. To my surprise Mr. Devoted's room stands empty.

"Where's Mr. D.?" I ask the floor administrator.

"D? Oh, he left yesterday. A room opened up at M——."

That is that, I realize. No farewells. No follow-up. I've been thinking of Mr. Charming's emotional welfare, but I too feel a sense of loss.

"You haven't see Mr. C., have you?" I ask the floor administrator.

"Oh, C. He's on the nurse-practitioner service, isn't he?" The administrator flips through a clipboard and shakes his head. "He went home yesterday too," he says. "We cleaned house, doctor."

"We sure did," I agree.

Lucy fills me in on the details later. The hospital decided that it did not wish to provide Mr. Charming with room and board for eternity, so a senior case manager ferreted out a long-term care facility, several hours away, which was willing to accept his "crummy" private insurance. These arrangements have been in the works for days, but nobody has told me, because I am no longer Mr. Charming's doctor. I do not know whether he has had an opportunity to exchange good-byes with Mr. Devoted. I do not know whether he has found his next girlfriend. Or even whether he is still alive.

I learn these details of Mr. Charming's departure from Lucy following morning rounds, but that is after I've had a moment to stand at the door to the bare room that he has shared with Mr. Devoted for the first twenty-seven days of my internship. This is how most stories end in the hospital. Not with crash carts and sirens and electric shocks to the chest, but with an empty room, a crisp white bed, silence. And already the rising murmur of distant life encroaches on me.

Livery

Every physician has a favorite patient, and mine, Mr. Nimble, was living out my own worst nightmare: he was perfectly healthy but unable to leave the hospital.* The trouble had started the previous morning, when the lanky, square-jawed ninety-four-year-old had stumbled on his daily walk to the grocery store. Soon he found himself in the emergency room of Manhattan's Mount Sinai Hospital, ankle sprained, knee bandaged, awaiting a series of routine blood tests. This was apparently when he had made his fatal mistake: he asked one of the medical residents if she would prescribe him what he called "a suicide pill" so that, should his health ever fail him, he

---

* In accordance with the Health Insurance Portability and Accountability Act of 1996 and the canons of medical confidentiality, some names and demographic data in this essay have been altered slightly to protect the identity of the subject.

would have an immediate means of escape. And that was how the ill-fated Mr. Nimble ended up behind the locked doors of a psychiatric ward, in oversized cotton pajamas, pleading with me, a junior headshrinker, for his freedom.

"I've learned my lesson," he promised. "No more stupid questions."

We were seated across the long wooden table in our evaluation room. I noticed that ST. LUKE'S HOSPITAL—the name of our crosstown competitor—was emblazoned above the breast pocket of Mr. Nimble's pajama top, a testament to the value of outsourcing laundry services. The shrink who had admitted Mr. Nimble overnight had documented concerns about the elderly man's memory and cognition—and this outfit certainly wasn't helping to orient him.

"I thought doctors could do that sort of thing these days," Mr. Nimble explained. "Honestly, I don't go to the doctor very often."

"When *was* the last time you saw a doctor?" I inquired.

"Let me see," he replied. "I suppose HST was still president."

"HST?"

"Harry S. Truman."

That resolved at least one mystery: if you went to the doctor only every sixty years, you might easily believe that physicians prescribe suicide pills.

"*Why* did you go to the doctor?"

Mr. Nimble shrugged. "I guess I was sick. . . ."

"You guess?"

"It was a long time ago." Mr. Nimble beamed a smile that melded bemusement and frustration. "Nobody told me to remember these things in case I ended up an old man and got myself tossed into the loony bin."

"But you remember that Harry Truman was president at the time?"

"Of course, I do," replied Mr. Nimble. "I was his chauffeur."

Here was one of those definitive moments in psychiatry that separate the trained professionals from the pretenders. I had learned this the hard way: during my first month of service, a bipolar patient had duped me into believing that his uncle was the prime minister of Canada. So I asked Mr. Nimble to tell me more about his relationship with the thirty-third president. If my patient revealed that he and HST had hatched the Marshall Plan together over the divider of a 1946 DeSoto or that he'd also spied for Moscow via transmitters in his molars, I'd have viewed his claims more critically.

"Not much to tell," said Mr. Nimble. "I was his chauffeur only when he came to New York City. I drove him to the airport several times—both when he was president and afterwards—and I remember waiting for him outside a hotel on Fifth Avenue. . . . Our fleet drove executives and movie stars too. My boss knew someone who knew someone. . . ."

"And what did you talk about with HST?"

"Talk? He hardly ever said a word to me," answered Mr. Nimble, his arthritic fingers laced together on the tabletop.

"Okay, that's not entirely true. Once, he wished me a Merry Christmas."

I imagine it is *possible* that Mr. Nimble was lying or exaggerating, that one of his colleagues had actually transported HST, for instance, but he'd assumed the credit. However, I instinctively believed every word that he'd said: the man exuded a plainspoken sturdiness that I associate with a more innocent era—a time when men sported hats outdoors and went about their lives in black-and-white. Whether or not the nonagenarian's claims proved true, they certainly did not qualify as delusions of grandeur. In fact Mr. Nimble looked the opposite of manic. He was as placid as a marble bust.

"Are you going to kill yourself?" I asked.

Mr. Nimble chewed over my question thoroughly. "No," he said.

"Do you feel depressed?"

"I didn't before I ended up in the loony bin."

I couldn't suppress a grin. "And now?"

Mr. Nimble shook his head. "How would *you* feel if *you* were in here?"

"Point taken," I replied. "I realize this is not an ideal situation."

My patient leaned forward and lowered his voice. "Don't take this the wrong way," he said, "but this place is full of crazy people."

Never has my work environment been described with such unvarnished clarity.

"Will you let me go home now?" Mr. Nimble asked. "At my age, every *hour* counts."

"I'm not in charge," I answered candidly. "I'll do the best I can."

If I have learned anything during the course of practicing psychiatry, it is that "the best I can" is often not good enough. This reality has proven particularly true when it comes to convincing my superiors to spring patients from the hospital. As anyone who has ever spent time inside the "loony bin" or even watched *One Flew over the Cuckoo's Nest* knows all too well, getting into the asylum is far easier than getting out. During the 1970s psychologist David Rosenhan conducted a series of experiments in which he demonstrated that psychiatric diagnosis is about as scientific as palm reading. In one experiment eight "pseudo-patients"—all in excellent mental health—hoodwinked doctors at hospitals across the country into admitting them to acute psych wards with diagnoses of either schizophrenia or bipolar disorder. In another study a leading hospital was warned that such "pseudo-patients" would soon be seeking admission—when none in fact was— and the institution's psychiatrists promptly diagnosed 41 of 193 prospective patients as likely impostors. What does this have to do with Mr. Nimble? In a system where nobody has any idea what they are doing, but where human lives are at stake, health-care providers have powerful incentives to err on the side of caution. If Mr. Nimble loses a few weeks of freedom, the thinking runs, this is clearly regrettable; if he leaves the hospital too soon and jumps from the Brooklyn Bridge or just forgets to switch off the gas range and blows his neighbors to smithereens, the liability will be deadly.

The gods of madness favored Mr. Nimble in one crucial respect. Not only did he have in me a junior psychiatrist who harbors grave doubts about involuntary confinement, but my boss, Dr. A., was among the most reasonable clinicians I have encountered during my time in inpatient care. Several years younger than I was and already the unit chief in geriatric psychiatry, she was by no means a pushover. Dr. A. possessed enough raw scientific knowledge to bulldoze her way through almost any argument, but she was a careful and open-minded listener. At the same time she never emerged from behind her dazzling and durable smile, so that after two months working alongside her, dawn to dusk, I knew absolutely nothing of her inner life, although I sensed—fairly or not—that alacrity and compassion were her personal armor against the great existential maw of human existence. Unfortunately for Mr. Nimble, Dr. A. had spotted the warning about "memory and cognition" in his admission note.

I found Dr. A. in the dayroom with the medical students. Behind her a manic patient was butchering Gershwin relentlessly on the ward's well-battered piano. My boss broke off her minilesson on the pharmacology of antipsychotic medications to ask me, "So what are we going to do with Mr. Nimble?"

"Send him home?" I ventured.

Dr. A. toyed with her pen. "I thought he was suicidal and cognitively impaired?"

That gave me an opportunity to relate Mr. Nimble's history, including his relationship with HST and his mistaken beliefs about suicide pills. I summed matters up with the line that I'd been stockpiling all morning: "Give me livery or give me death." Dr. A. did not laugh. One of the medical students winced.

"Sometimes a request like that can be a cry for help," said Dr. A. As reasonable as my boss was, she was also a psychiatrist. "Does he seem depressed?"

"He's happier than I am."

I wasn't sure if Dr. A. interpreted my answer as a yes or a no.

"Let's go see him," she suggested.

Her offer was not as promising at it sounded. In psychiatry the rules are largely inflexible. The facts, on the other hand, are often highly subjective. For junior headshrinkers like me, this affords a source of empowerment. If I were to tell Dr. A. that I believed the practice of involuntarily committing cognitively impaired patients to be unethical, she'd likely have rolled her eyes. In contrast, if I informed her that Mr. Nimble had the memory of an elephant, my testimony might lead to his discharge. Once Dr. A. had empirical evidence of her own, however, my powers would diminish quickly.

We encountered Mr. Nimble standing in the corridor, arms folded across his chest, looking rather like a disappointed track coach waiting at a finish line. I introduced him to Dr. A., and he clasped her hand.

"Are you ready to let me go home?" he asked.

Dr. A. responded with her impenetrable smile. "We just want to make sure it's *safe* for you to go home," she assured him. "Who lives with you at home?"

"Nobody," answered Mr. Nimble.

"Do you have friends or family nearby?"

Mr. Nimble frowned. "No friends. No family."

"A neighbor?" pressed Dr. A. "Anyone?"

"Not anymore," said Mr. Nimble. "They're all gone."

I wanted to call a time-out, to coach Mr. Nimble on his answers. Even if he concocted a relative, I could pretend to have spoken to this person—a white lie that my conscience would gladly tolerate—but the man wasn't yielding any material for me to work with. It is nearly impossible to escape from the loony bin if you don't have someone to vouch for you on the outside. I anticipated Dr. A.'s next question, knowing that it might seal Mr. Nimble's destiny.

"Is there somebody you can call in an emergency?"

"Can't call anybody," said Mr. Nimble. "I don't have a telephone."

"Why don't you have a phone?" asked Dr. A.

"What do I need a telephone for? I don't have anybody to call."

I actually had to bite my lip to keep from laughing. The medical student who'd winced at my livery quip looked to be on the verge of a guffaw.

Dr. A. changed the subject. "How is your memory?"

"Not too good," Mr. Nimble answered candidly. "But I'm ninety-four. How good does it have to be?"

"What did you have for breakfast yesterday?" asked Dr. A.

"For breakfast?" echoed Mr. Nimble. "That's a very good question."

"What do you *usually* have for breakfast?"

A furrow appeared beneath Mr. Nimble's shiny pate. "Goodness. That's also a very good question," he said. "Can you ask me again later?"

Later. That became Mr. Nimble's signature response. *Later* he would tell us where he did his shopping, what shows he watched on television. As I had feared, the deeper we delved, the less he appeared to recall. "It all makes sense when I'm at home," he explained. "My brain doesn't know how to get to the store, but my feet still do."

"Wise feet" no doubt served Mr. Nimble quite well in the outside world, but there is no provision for "limb cognition" in psychiatry's diagnostic manual. Similarly Dr. A. appeared unimpressed that Mr. Nimble remembered how much he owed in monthly rent only when the landlord slid the bill under his door.

"Can we call your landlord?" she asked.

"Honestly, ma'am, we don't get along so well," said Mr. Nimble. "He's going to tell you that I'm senile because he wants me out of my apartment—so he can rent it to someone else for more money."

"What's his name?" I inquired.

Mr. Nimble shrugged. "Ask me later."

Our interview ended shortly afterward when one of the nurse's aides summoned my patient for lunch. I followed Dr. A. into a nearby conference room. Much like theatergoers reflecting upon a play, we make a point in psychiatry to keep a healthy distance between our patients and our discussions of them. As soon as the door to the conference room clicked shut, I launched my strongest argument. "Okay, so the man isn't going to win any memory contests," I conceded. "But he says he was doing fine on his own. He looks well-nourished. Let's face it: if he hadn't twisted his ankle, he'd still be living at home, and nobody would have any idea how impaired he is."

Dr. A. listened patiently. "We should do some formal memory testing," she announced. "At the very least, he needs help during the day. Maybe a visiting nurse. What if he'd fallen in his apartment instead of on the street? He could be lying there right now with a twisted ankle—or a broken hip—and he doesn't even own a phone."

A visiting nurse or a home health aide struck me as an excellent idea. After one morning I already knew Mr. Nimble well enough to realize that he wasn't going to agree.

"And if he won't *accept* a visiting nurse?" I asked.

"He can't go home alone like this," said Dr. A. "In the outpatient clinic, we had a patient like that who accidentally set his apartment on fire. If he won't accept any help, we're going to have to start thinking about guardianship, possibly assisted-living. What other options do we have? I'm open to suggestions. . . ."

So much, I thought, for doing the best that I could.

I do not mean to portray Dr. A. as the villain of this tragedy or myself as the hero, for that matter. The choices and trade-offs are far too complex for that. The chilling reality was that Mr. Nimble *was* perfectly capable of forgetting to turn off a teapot or a faucet—only one memory lapse away from endangering unsuspecting strangers. *All of us,* of course, are capable of such slipups; in Mr. Nimble's case, the odds of a calamity were simply greater. The underlying problem is that our society has never had a meaningful, collective conversation regarding how much risk a mildly impaired senior citizen must pose to his neighbors before we take away his freedom. As ethical conundrums go, this one is a doozy. A priori, we all have the potential to find ourselves old and isolated like feisty Mr. Nimble, clinging to our remaining strands of independence and dignity. Needless to say, some of us may also end up living next door to such an individual—and a few unlucky souls among us will become those rare bystanders blown to oblivion. How have we, as a nation, addressed this dilemma? We've foisted the burden onto geriatricians and psychiatrists, to be decided piecemeal, if and when people like Mr. Nimble stumble their way to the attention of the health-care system. I should note that our society also hasn't engaged meaningfully in a second, related dialogue about how much peril a man like Mr. Nimble must pose *to himself* before we force him into supervised living—but here, as an admitted outlier on the subject of patient autonomy, I find myself willing to tolerate almost any level of risk.

That evening, feeling as though I'd failed Mr. Nimble, I snuck off the ward via the back exit, dreading the moment when I'd have to tell him that his future autonomy was in jeopardy. Before rounds the next morning, Alice—the earthy, strong-willed psychiatric social worker whom I harbored a secret crush on—cornered me behind the nurse's station. Under ordinary circumstances a moment alone with her would have made the entire workday worthwhile, but I already knew that Alice had been assigned to coordinate Mr. Nimble's discharge plan. Or, in this instance, his lack of a discharge plan. Alice grabbed my forearm—her distinctive method of gaining my attention—and gave me a look to tarnish brass.

"Nimble," she said. "I heard you want to send him home!"

"With a visiting nurse," I offered. "With a home health aide."

Alice released my arm. "And he doesn't have a goddam telephone? What is he going to do if his building catches on fire?"

"Exactly what anybody else would do. He'll run outside," I replied. "Who makes phone calls in the middle of a fire?"

"I can't send a guy home without a telephone. I could lose my license."

I wanted to point out that human beings had survived for millions of years without telephones, that more than one billion people across the globe *still* lived without phone access. But Alice was no run-of-the-ward adversary, and remaining in her good graces was as important to me as winning Mr. Nimble's freedom.

"And just so you know, he's not interested in a visiting nurse or a home health aide . . . or even going to a senior center," added Alice. "He's an absolute disaster."

"*I'm* going to be worse than that someday," I shot back. "They're going to wheel me through those double doors, and I'm not going to remember what I had for breakfast, or who's buried in Grant's Tomb, and you're going to ship me off to some glue factory with the other dimwits. My day is coming soon enough. . . ."

Alice was sashaying up the corridor before I'd even finished.

"Disaster," she repeated as she fled. "Total disaster."

That was my cue to hunt down Mr. Nimble—not too challenging a feat on a locked ward of twenty elderly head cases—and to convince him to compromise. Once he'd left the hospital, as far as I was concerned, he could slam his door on the visiting nurse or aide. All he had to do was pledge that he'd let her in for now—prevaricate, if you will—and then vanish into a city of eight million anonymous people, beyond the long arm of Dr. A. and the well-intentioned minions of the Mount Sinai Hospital.

Tracking Mr. Nimble proved even easier than I had imagined: I found him standing in precisely the same spot as he had been the afternoon before. His arms remained crossed, his expression placid. Seen from a distance, immobile and lost in reflection, he might have passed for a wax replica of himself.

"You," he greeted me. "Will you let me out of here?"

"I'm working on it," I pledged.

"I hope so," he said. "I'm not getting any younger."

I reminded Mr. Nimble that whether to discharge him was not entirely my decision and explained that some other staff members had concerns for his safety. "It doesn't help that you don't own a telephone," I informed him. "What would you do if you fell in your apartment and you broke your hip?"

Mr. Nimble flashed me a look of genuine pity, as though I was the one whose cognition stood in doubt. "I'd shout for help," he said. "What else should I do?"

"You'd shout for help," I repeated.

"We've got thin walls. The neighbors would hear me. Lord knows, I hear them!" he elaborated. "Whether they'd actually help me is another matter. . . ."

I chose this moment to pay lip service to my Hippocratic obligations. "You do realize that they might not hear you," I observed. "You could lie there on the floor in pain . . . and you might even die. . . . If you lived with other people, let's say in an assisted-living facility, that would be much less likely to happen. . . ."

"I'd be less likely to die?" he asked—expressionless.

I couldn't tell whether or not he was making fun of me.

"Of a broken hip," I said. "You'd be less likely to die of a broken hip."

He nodded. "Okay, then I'd die of something else. I'm ninety-four." The prospect of dying didn't appear to faze my patient—not nearly as much as the idea of staying on the psychiatric ward. "Why are we talking about this?"

I took a deep breath. "I'm going to do my best to help you get out of here," I told him. "But you're going to have to meet me halfway. I know you don't want a home health aide or a visiting nurse—"

"What do I need that for?"

"I know you don't *want* one. And once you leave here, nobody is going to force you to *keep* one. But later this afternoon, a woman is going to ask you if you're willing to have a home health aide for a few hours each day, and if you tell her that you are, it's much more likely that you'll be discharged. Of course, if later you change your mind . . . once you're home. . . ." I finished my sentence with a shrug.

Mr. Nimble digested my proposal slowly, as through gnawing the sinew off a lamb chop, until a glimmer of recognition finally appeared in his dark eyes. "So all I have to do is *say* I want a home health aide," he said. "That's a good one."

"I know it is," I agreed.

I didn't have much opportunity to savor my victory. A commotion erupted at the opposite end of the ward—another patient, a demented ex-seamstress, had slipped in the bathroom—and I had to coordinate an emergency CT scan of the woman's head and then document the details of that incident before returning to Mr. Nimble. The chauffeur had managed to acquire a cup of water since my departure, which he sipped through a cocktail straw, but—as though drawn by some unseen magnetic force—he'd returned to the precise spot where I'd left him.

"It's quite a place you have here," he said. "Never a dull moment."

"We should sell tickets," I agreed.

"Tickets." Mr. Nimble grinned broadly. "I like that."

"On the subject of things you might like," I continued, "I have one more proposition for you, and then I promise I'll leave you alone. How would you feel about going to a senior citizen center once or twice a week? . . . You could play cards, watch television. . . . Maybe make some new friends. . . ."

I was sincere in this proposal—the one suggestion I thought he might accept.

Mr. Nimble waved away the idea with his hand. "I'm too old for new friends. Besides, what do I want to spend my time with a pack of old folks for?"

"All right," I conceded. "I just wanted to put the option on the table."

"And I thank you for doing that," replied Mr. Nimble.

I'd done my darnedest, I told myself. My conscience was clear.

"I'm going to stop bothering you now, Mr. Nimble," I concluded. "Let's just go over our plan one more time. What are you going to say when the social worker comes back to ask you about a home health aide? What are you supposed to tell her?"

Mr. Nimble looked puzzled. "I don't think I understand," he said.

I tried again. "Sometime this afternoon, a social worker named Alice is going to ask you whether you'd like to have a home health aide come to your apartment. I know you don't want an aide, but I also know that you want to go home as soon as possible. Now we just discussed a plan for how you're going to answer her question. So when Alice asks you about the home health aide, what are you going to tell her?"

Mr. Nimble rubbed his chin thoughtfully.

"That's a good one," he said. "You'd better ask me later."

The day didn't get any better—Mr. Nimble again told Alice that he had no interest in a home health aide—and the following morning, the start of Mr. Nimble's fourth day in the hospital, matters even took a turn for the worse. Zeke, the medical student who'd winced at my humor, completed Mr. Nimble's formal cognitive testing. If I'd secretly hoped for the chauffeur to perform better on paper than he did in person, I was sadly disappointed. "Is his score really *that* bad?" I pressed Zeke. "Some of those questions are difficult. Did you give him the benefit of the doubt?"

"I offered him hints for every question."

"What about extra points for good luck?"

Zeke, a former professional hockey player, smiled politely. "I do have an idea for Mr. Nimble," he proposed. "Why don't we buy him a disposable cell phone for emergencies? I could pick one up at Radio Shack for thirty dollars."

I had no idea that anyone manufactured disposable cell phones—I still don't own a cell phone myself—but Zeke, a far savvier young man than I will ever be, assured me that these devices were ubiquitous. Didn't I know anything about drug dealing? About international terrorism? Alas, I did not. But if disposable phones were good enough for Al-Qaeda and the Latin Kings, I decided, they'd be good enough for Mr. Nimble. Predictably Mr. Nimble was at best reluctantly amenable to the idea—if it cost him absolutely nothing and if he didn't have to open an account of any sort.

We pitched the plan at morning rounds. Dr. A. warmed to it quickly. In addition to proving an ethical minefield, the lengthy process of forcing an unwilling patient into a nursing home was an economic drain on the hospital—the sort of burden that unit chiefs and medical directors will strain every muscle to avoid.

"It's not ideal," she acknowledged, "but at least he'll be better off than before."

I could sense that Alice and her supervisor, the director of psychiatric social work, were less impressed with this solution, but all I was asking of them was acquiescence. That much, it appeared, they could muster. So while I scrambled to complete Mr. Nimble's discharge paperwork, Zeke raced downtown to purchase the man a disposable phone. It was a Friday, I recall, and if we couldn't get the poor fellow out the door by five o'clock, he would be stuck on the ward through the weekend.

As with many dilemmas in psychiatry, our solution didn't solve the essential problem. In actuality our answer didn't even address it. Owning a cell phone wasn't going to improve Mr. Nimble's memory or decrease the likelihood that he'd leave the oven on by mistake or do anything to insulate his neighbors from his mental lapses. Arguably a cellular phone might help him if he fell at home and fractured a hip—but only if he could reach the device and could remember how to use it, neither of which seemed particularly likely. The truth of the matter was that we weren't treating Mr. Nimble at all. We were treating ourselves. We'd stumbled upon an ingenious, somewhat illogical way to convince ourselves that we had done something tangible to improve the life of an old man who didn't want our help in the first place. I have no doubt that Kafka would be proud of our achievement.

I cannot express how pained I was when Zeke returned empty-handed.

"So here's the problem," he explained. "It turns out they don't make disposable cell phones that last longer than three months. If you want to keep your phone longer than that, you have to buy a real one. It makes sense: why in the world would anyone want a permanent disposable cell phone?"

"Drug dealers might," I suggested. "Terrorists might."

I called Dr. A. in her private office and explained our predicament. "Do you want me to send Zeke back downtown for a three-month phone?" I asked.

"What's the point?" asked Dr. A. "That's not a long-term solution."

He's ninety-four, I thought. How long-term a solution do we need?

"I still think we should send him home," I ventured. "I'll document that we went to great lengths to offer him services, but he was unwilling, and that he's agreed to return to the hospital if he feels depressed or his memory gets worse."

A person could live ninety-four years in the silence that ensued. I have no idea what my boss was thinking about during that interval—whether she was reassessing the state of Mr. Nimble's cognition, envisioning the stress of having to tell her own boss that we were petitioning for guardianship, or reminiscing about an elderly loved one of her own who'd ended his days in a nursing facility. Perhaps Dr. A. was thinking about something else entirely: her dinner plans, when to feed her parking meter. I was afraid to ask. I'll likely never know.

"Okay," Dr. A. finally said. "He can go home."

"Today?" I asked—somewhat incredulous. "Right now?"

"We did the best we could," she said. "What else are we supposed to do?"

Mr. Nimble didn't look a day over ninety in his street clothes. He had changed into a button-down shirt and beige trousers in preparation for his discharge, and one of the nurse's aides was helping him feed the laces back into his shoes. I shook the man's hand, as I do with all my departing patients, and wished him well. I also asked if he would be willing to let me write an essay about him in the future, so that other people might be aware of his experience. That clearly struck the old man as a highly amusing proposition. For the first time in four days, he broke into a laugh.

"You write whatever you want," he said. "But don't ask me to read it."

"I won't," I agreed. And then, on impulse, I asked, "Do you want to hear a joke?"

"Sure," said Mr. Nimble. "Nothing wrong with a joke."

So I shared the only joke I know that involves chauffeurs. In the joke the pope asks his driver if they can trade places for the afternoon. Unfortunately the pope's steering skills prove limited, and he is soon stopped by a dumbfounded police officer. That officer radios his chief to explain that he has pulled over a vehicle only to discover that the occupant is too important to ticket. "Who is this guy who's so important?" asks the chief. "I don't know who he is," responds the officer, "but the pope is his chauffeur."

"That's a good one," said Mr. Nimble. "The pope is his chauffeur."

As a junior headshrinker, I often feel like the cop in that joke, but this is not a notion that I chose to share with Mr. Nimble. He was ninety-four years old, after all, an age when—as he frequently reminded me—every hour counts. He didn't need to squander any more time reflecting upon his psychiatric experience.

"Good luck to you," I said. "I'm glad you're going home."

"I am too. I sure am," said Mr. Nimble. "Don't take this the wrong way, but I hope I never see any of you again."

"Likewise," I said. "Please be a stranger."

And then the double doors opened, and Mr. Nimble, my favorite patient, vanished forever into the sea of human madness.

Our Incredible Shrinking Discourse

I received my first death threat on March 5, 2009. I'd logged into my home computer after a long workday at the hospital, hoping for an email message from the comedic actress who was my crush du jour. Instead I discovered a flurry of symposia announcements and reprint requests and—at the very bottom of my screen—a personal message from an unfamiliar email account. The content contained a reply to an article that I had recently written for an obscure website, in which I had argued that couples using taxpayer dollars to fund in vitro fertilization should be required to test their embryos for potentially fatal genetic diseases. That's a relatively controversial viewpoint in my professional field, bioethics, yet not exactly a casus belli, or even a voting issue, for ordinary Americans.

My correspondent, "Hazmanx99," cogently expressed his (or her) concern that mandatory genetic screening was the moral equivalent of Hitler's efforts to euthanize the disabled. There was no mistaking, or forgetting, Hazmanx99's animus: I rarely receive messages that begin with the salutation "You Nazi Fuck" and conclude with vivid descriptions of my impending dismemberment.

My initial instinct was to answer Hazmanx99—to explain that, far from wishing to kill off those with disabilities, I have for years advocated on their behalf. After all I did not relish the prospect of a total stranger believing me a genocidal maniac. So I penned a friendly missive, intending to disarm my mysterious nemesis with a blend of logic, humility and good cheer. I confess that in my naïveté I fantasized that we might eventually achieve a rapprochement in the spirit of Norman Mailer and William Styron. I even included a light-hearted postscript: "Why '99'? Are there ninety-eight other 'Hazmanxes'? And what is the plural of 'Hazmanx' anyway?" I never heard back.

I wish I could report that my "encounter" with the ninety-ninth Hazmanx was an isolated incident. Instead he or she proved to be a pioneer. When I started publishing a regular ethics column in the *Huffington Post* later that spring, I found myself inundated with email—and occasional "snail mail"— distinguished by varying degrees of hostility. Some of these messages seemed genuinely amusing in their irony, such as a short note I received from a "pro-life" abortion opponent named Mike Kanavel who wrote that "I hope you fucking choke on your own vomit in your sleep." Others were more alarming, primarily because their authors should have known better, such as a diatribe from disbarred attorney and perennial Washington state political candidate Stan Lippmann, entitled "Nazi Moron Scumbag," who cautioned that "half of all Americans" were ready to string me up as a "genocidal War Criminal [sic]." Admittedly the topics that I address can be contentious: not merely abortion and assisted suicide, but fetal organ donation and bestiality and reproductive cloning. However, only a minority of the nine bona fide threats of physical violence that I've received actually relate to topics that I would ever have expected to inflame passions. By far the most frightening message to appear in my inbox—and the only time that I've seriously considered contacting the police—came from a man irate that I'd opined in favor of fluoridating the water supply.

I have made a point of keeping these threats in perspective. I am an utterly minor intellectual, after all—or possibly even, as one ex-girlfriend pointedly informed me, an utterly minor *pseudo*-intellectual. If someone truly wants to strike a blow against entrenched liberalism, they're going to go after Noam Chomsky or Gloria Steinem—not an armchair philosopher who publishes jargon-laced articles in the *Journal of Bioethical Inquiry* and the *Cambridge Quarterly of Healthcare Ethics*. One of my dearest friends, an authority on Iranian-American relations, encouraged me to expunge my apartment's address and telephone number from the Internet before some unhinged lunatic appeared upon my stoop. *If you're not willing to protect yourself,* he warned, *consider your innocent neighbors.*

Needless to say, such excessive privacy has a downside. It is not that I fear "letting the terrorists win," so to speak. I am fully reconciled to my own cowardice, deeply proud of my preference for self-preservation over principle. What I am unwilling to do is to forgo the letters that I receive from individuals who *agree* with me or, more important, who have sincere questions about my views. These have included, on two occasions, handwritten queries from elderly correspondents who have read my articles in the public library but, lacking computer savvy and email accounts, have asked the librarian to look up my postal address online. This pair of notes was worth all the stress of being ordered by an irate correspondent "never to show [my] ugly face" in the state of Kentucky. Besides, I reassured myself, threatening someone over the Internet isn't *really* threatening them, is it? It's more akin to online sex—which an increasing number of spouses do not appear to view as cheating. After all, cyberspace envelops a person like an alcoholic stupor, simultaneously inflaming and disinhibiting. Who hasn't written something in an email message that he or she would never have uttered face to face? For all I knew, the ninety-ninth Hazmanx, whose tag name increasingly reminded me of an apocalyptic prophet, was in fact an elderly, churchgoing widow on the Isle of Man . . . about to celebrate her centennial.

Then the package arrived: a box the size of a toaster, wrapped in brown paper. I returned home from a New Year's party to find the nondescript parcel resting on my welcome mat. No card. No return address. Just my name, scrawled with black Magic Marker across the side in the bold lettering of a child or a psychopath. I carried the parcel into my apartment—it felt too heavy for its bulk, like a dead cat— and I was on the verge of opening it, when I noticed a strand of wire poking through the side. I inspected the wire momentarily: it was a twisted, copper-colored strip of metal—how the end of a coat hanger might appear after being unfolded to open a locked car door. Or, it suddenly struck me, this was what a makeshift explosive might look like.

I had written a column earlier that day in which I urged that the "age of consent" be reduced to the age of sixteen. I now wondered whether some deranged opponent of teenage sexuality had left me a "parting gift" in protest. Or was this payback for my earlier defense of an open-borders immigration policy? Simultaneously another portion of my brain insisted that I was reacting irrationally, that the package might just as easily be a gift from a neighbor or a forgotten purchase from eBay. I didn't have the confidence to call the police and report the parcel as suspicious, but I also lacked the courage to open the box and risk losing a hand. So I chose a middle course; I hurled the package across my apartment with full force. If it were a bomb, I reasoned, a collision with the far wall would either incapacitate the device—or the ensuing explosion, at the opposite end of the room, was less likely to injure me. That was utterly asinine, of course. As I've subsequently learned, a well-made bomb that size could easily have taken down the entire ceiling. But, to my relief, the package did not detonate.

I tentatively retrieved the package. A pungent liquid seeped through the gash around the wire—and I recoiled at the smell. I will never shake the indelible memory of realizing that, instead of a bomb, I'd been sent acid. Wasn't that the weapon of choice that fundamentalists used against women in Iraq and Pakistan? Seconds later, of course, I recognized the aroma. Wine! Closer inspection of the now-dripping package revealed shards of glass and a sopping card. One of my former writing students had hand delivered two bottles of cabernet in a wire basket.

Our intellectual discourse is contracting.

What I mean to express by this expansive declaration is actually two distinct phenomena that are all too often conflated by free-thought advocates. The more obvious concern is that the robust exchange of conflicting ideas, so essential to social progress, has been dampened by the rise of ad hominem attacks in nearly every academic and cultural discipline. Increasingly we engage with only people who agree with us. Those who disagree are not merely mistaken—but downright evil. Technological advances, such as the Internet, which in theory offer the potential of increased dialogue, have instead largely become forums for polarized attack and vitriolic counterattack. As soon as our mouths open, our minds close.

A second concern—one largely ignored by the media—is that the actual breadth and variety of ideas acceptable in public conversation is beginning to narrow. After a half century of liberalization in the United States and Western Europe, during which previously taboo subjects entered the forum of debate, particularly in the fields of human sexuality and bioethics, our range of discourse now actually appears to be contracting. Having broken down a millennium of moral barriers in the course of one generation, we seem to have increasingly accepted that certain remaining barriers should not be broken. On subjects ranging from neonatal euthanasia and eugenics to child pornography and Holocaust revisionism, we have concluded—to our own detriment—that some ideas should not be expressed at all.

The demonization of Princeton University's Peter Singer, and his response, offers a case study in how these two distinct phenomena can coalesce. Professor Singer, whether one admires or abhors his uncompromising utilitarian outlook, is the most significant philosopher of our era. I do not think it's a stretch to contend that one must look back several centuries—before Freud, before Marx, possibly as long ago as Immanuel Kant—to find a thinker who reshaped the intellectual landscape of his age so rapidly and so comprehensively. Singer has written passionately for the rights of animals and traveled the globe crusading against poverty. However, he may be best known for what is arguably his most controversial view, first annunciated in *Practical Ethics,* that terminating the lives of severely disabled newborns may, under certain circumstances, be both ethical and desirable. The outcry against Singer that has followed him since he first expressed this view in the late 1970s has been intense, personal, and often violent. Its most dramatic moment, which Singer has himself written about extensively, occurred at the University of Zurich in 1989, when enraged disability rights advocates forcibly prevented him from delivering a lecture. Rather than challenging Singer's ideas with their own, which he welcomed them to do, these protesters sought to drive his ideas underground. Neonatal euthanasia is a concept so dangerous, they believed, it could not be tolerated long enough to refute its justification on the merits. In short, by refusing to engage in debate, Singer's opponents attempted to shrink the public discourse.

Much has been written about the ugly campaign against Professor Singer. I say against Singer—not against his ideas. Figures as diverse as libertarian publisher Steven Forbes and Marc Maurer of the National Federation of the Blind argued against his appointment to the Princeton faculty and sought his intellectual ostracism, suggestions meant more to stifle him than to prove his ideas wrong. What has been largely overlooked is the subtle success of this campaign. Singer has not retracted his opinions, nor has Princeton retracted his tenure. At the same time, he no longer hard pedals his views on personhood. Instead he has devoted his later writings to charitable donation and the horrors of poverty. I doubt Professor Singer would agree that he has been "silenced." As an independent (and admiring) observer, I cannot help believing that he has been "tempered" by his detractors. That moderation is certainly understandable: as a practical matter, emphasizing this one controversial view threatened his opportunity to champion other causes of great value. (Lost to many of his opponents was the possibility that they might disagree with Singer on one issue, but agree with him on others.) Alas the result is that neonatal euthanasia lost its intellectual champion. Equally disturbing to note, others in the field of moral philosophy have been reluctant to embrace Singer's views on the matter—at least publicly. I know of several bioethicists who have privately expressed to me their sympathy toward Singer's theory of personhood—but refuse to do so openly for fear of the backlash.

I do not mean to suggest, in highlighting Singer's case, that ideas of only one particular ideology have been driven from the communal square. When I first started teaching at Brown University a decade ago, an uproar ensued over the decision of the student newspaper to publish a highly controversial advertisement by conservative provocateur David Horowitz titled "Ten Reasons Why Reparations for Blacks Is a Bad Idea for Blacks—and Racist Too." Among the premises advanced by Horowitz was the argument that "trillions of dollars in transfer payments have been made to African-Americans in the form of welfare benefits and racial preferences" since the 1960s, eliminating any need for affirmative action, and that African Americans should be grateful to whites for their freedom and "high standard of living." Several student groups responded by "appropriating" (some might say stealing) the entire run of the *Brown Daily Herald.* As someone who disagrees with all ten of

Horowitz's reasons, and his worldview more generally, I found this act of civil disobedience appalling, but not, as many of my colleagues did, because theft is inherently wrong or immoral. Rather my concern was that by removing Horowitz's ideas from the public debate—however misguided I might think them—one ceded the intellectual and moral vigor that would have come with refuting them. In other words those who sought to silence Horowitz, rather than challenging his case on the merits, were also silencing themselves. Unlike Professor Singer, Horowitz has not since been tempered in his views. At the same time, he has drifted from the "mainstream" to a position where he now attacks the liberal intelligentsia, rather than attempting to engage with it. That is our loss as much as his.

Unfortunately ideas are dangerous. The judges who voted to execute Socrates understood this, as did the Genevese elders who expelled Calvin. Our better selves would prefer to believe in the efficiency of the "marketplace of ideas"—that idealistic notion, often attributed to Supreme Court Justice Oliver Wendell Holmes Jr., that if philosophies and ideologies compete freely, the most worthy thoughts will gain acceptance. At the same time, in our more cynical moments, we recognize the Orwellian truth that, if you can take away the words for expressing an idea and the public forum in which to promote it, you can eventually eradicate the idea itself. In free societies that is the inherent tension that governs disputes over the right to uncensored speech. What if the "wrong" ideas prove persuasive? Can we risk allowing the Holocaust deniers or the flat-earthers their say? Should we allow those who oppose free expression to use our liberties against us? Increasingly, over the past two decades, we have answered NO. Occasionally western nations have resorted to raw political force—such as Ireland's new blasphemy statute or the nineteen-year-old French ban on "inciting religious and racial hatred" that has repeatedly been used to fine Brigitte Bardot. Far more often, however, legal action has been unnecessary. All that has been required is an increasing unwillingness—in the universities, in the media, in our daily lives—to engage with ideas that we do not like. We no longer need fatwas or royal edicts to tell us not to speak or think subversively. Most of us manage to avoid doing so with little effort.

New York University psychologist Jonathan Haidt has built a career designing moral scenarios that provoke audiences to strong responses that they cannot rationally defend—a process he terms "moral dumbfounding." The most famous of these involves a hypothetical case of consensual incest: "Julie and Mark are siblings vacationing together in the south of France. One night, after a lovely day spent exploring the local countryside, they share a delicious dinner and a few bottles of red wine. One thing leads to another and Julie and Mark decide to have sex. Although she's on the pill, Mark uses a condom just in case. They enjoy themselves very much, but decide not to have sex again. The siblings promise to keep the one-night affair secret and discover, over time, that having sex brought them even closer together. Did Julie and Mark do something wrong?"

According to Haidt, most people *do* believe the siblings acted wrongly. However, the reasons that they offer to explain this judgment—"the risk of having kids with genetic abnormalities" and "that sex will damage the sibling relationship"—are overtly incompatible with the stated scenario, which includes multiple forms of birth control and a closer familial bond. The problem revealed here is not simply that people don't read as carefully as they should. What is alarming is that, because the ethics of consensual incest are largely outside the bounds of polite discussion, most people who oppose such relations cannot explain why they hold their views. I do not intend to endorse brother-sister sex. Nor, for that matter, am I staking out a position against it. My concern is that enlightened adults should be able to debate the question intelligently. Otherwise we risk mistaking the familiar for the moral.

The most dangerous ideas are not those that challenge the status quo. The most dangerous ideas are those so embedded in the status quo, so wrapped in a cloud of inevitability, that we forget they are ideas at all. When we forget that the underpinnings of our society are conscious choices, we become woefully unable to challenge those choices. We also become ill equipped to defend them.

Euripides exhorted his audiences: "Question everything. Learn something. Answer nothing."

My favorite exercise, when teaching bioethics, is to ask my students to list ten questions that "cannot be asked" in contemporary America. As an example, I write on the chalkboard: "Why shouldn't admission to elite colleges and universities be auctioned off to the highest bidders?" I have found that the very question infuriates some Ivy Leaguers so much that they want to debate it immediately, rather than listing other objectionable inquiries. Soon my most promising students are formulating questions of their own: "Should smart people be paid to have more babies?" "What's wrong with exposing children to pornography?" "Is patriotism immoral?" I am consistently amazed and impressed with the ability of my students to challenge social norms and moral conventions—when doing so as part of a classroom exercise. I am not confident that many of them continue to pose such questions over the dinner table.

Which leads me back to Hazmanx99. The real harm done by the Hazmanxes, Mike Kanavals, and Stan Lippmanns of the world is that they inevitably make me less likely to engage with those who share their views and disagree with mine. The automated reply to Peter Singer's email reads: "Many people send me messages with questions about, or comments on, my views. Although I read all such messages, I regret that I rarely have time to reply to them." I suspect, after enough overt threats, he also lacks the inclination. At the same time, much as a person never forgets his or her first love, first job, or first encounter with illness, I find my first authentic death threat will always hold a special place in my heart. To me it is a reminder that, unless we continue to pose indecent questions and to raise taboo subjects, we are liable to find ourselves thinking "outside the box" of acceptable thought—without having moved at all. That is a far greater threat to our moral welfare than all the radical bioethicists and right-wing provocateurs and anonymous cyberspace bullies combined.

Or I could be wrong.

Divided Expectations

I am approaching my half-life.

According to the most recent data from the United States Department of Health and Human Services, the average American now lives 77.9 years, which places our mean half-life at approximately 38 years, 11 months, and 12 days. That is discouragingly short when compared to uranium ($t\frac{1}{2}$ = 4.47 billion years), but an eternity by the standards of the mayfly ($t\frac{1}{2}$ < 12 hrs.) or the morning-glory blossom ($t\frac{1}{2}$ < 4 hrs.). Assuming I myself prove average—and I can boast a well-established track record for mediocrity—I will arrive at my own half-life on February 2, 2013, around three o'clock in the afternoon. From that moment forward, I'll be more history than future. Afterwards I may suffer existential remorse—buy a crimson Corvette Stingray, elope with an eighteen-year-old au pair—but *technically*, it will be too late for a *mid*-life crisis.

Of course, I might *not* be average. I may be middling in most respects, but when it comes to truly high stakes matters —romance, automotive safety—I have a tendency to underperform. So I could already be more than halfway toward my expiration date, clinging to the shorter strand of my mortal coil, obliviously puttering my way down the back nine. The problem with human half-lives is that they can be calculated only in retrospect. Who could have imagined that twelve-year-old James Dean, opening gates for an uncle's tractor on his Indiana homestead, had already bought more than half the farm? Or that John F. Kennedy had eclipsed his halfway mark as a senior at Harvard? For the overly optimistic, one also has the example of French supercentenarian Jeanne Calment (1875–1997), who had more life ahead of her than behind her at retirement age. Relying on the law of averages often turns perilous, a lesson learned dramatically by attorney André-François Raffray, who agreed to pay Mrs. Calment 2,500 francs monthly in 1965—when she turned ninety—in return for the deed to her apartment on her death. After Raffray's own demise in 1995, his widow (presumably "in for a centime, in for a franc") continued the annuity payments, which ultimately totaled twice the value of the flat. In short pacing oneself, difficult enough during bike rides or foreplay, becomes a Herculean challenge when one does not know in advance what interval one has been allotted. That is likely why so many folks exceed their lifetime allocation for cheesecake. If there is an afterlife, it is undoubtedly brimming with Monday-morning quarterbacks.

My own half-life serves not merely as a flashing neon announcement that time is running short, but also a reminder of all the accomplishments now beyond my grasp. I will not become a Rhodes Scholar (maximum age = 26 yrs.) or a member of the Swiss Guard (max starting age [msa] = 30 yrs.) or a New York City police officer (msa = 35 yrs.). My chance to serve as an FBI special agent (msa = 37 yrs.) is gone. Even with gender reassignment surgery, I have no shot at being crowned Miss America (max = 25 yrs.). In addition many doors have been closed, not by rules, but by reality: I am unlikely to play shortstop for the New York Yankees or join the Astronaut Corp or make out with my teenage crush (now happily married) in the backseat of a car. No elderly relative will ever mention my potential, unless in reference to an objective unfulfilled. If I do attend a high school prom again, it will be as a chaperone. While I suppose I should take solace in the knowledge that I can still join the French Foreign Legion (msa = 40 yrs.) and eventually the AARP, my opportunities for accomplishment have rapidly dwindled. As my favorite high school teacher used to say (before he died prematurely of a brain aneurysm), "When you reach middle age, you have to divide your expectations in half." His mistake—a common one, I have discovered—was placing "middle age" on the far side of sixty, rather than the near side of forty.

The human lifespan is far shorter than we think it is. Average life expectancy is itself a misleading statistic, as it actually applies to children born today. So while an infant born in 2012 can expect to live to 77.9 years, my own prospects are likely somewhat shorter. That 77.9 figure also does not take into account my gender or the roughly 300,000 Newport cigarettes that I smoked before my craving for pleasure succumbed to my fear of sudden death. Basically, I am deluding myself. I like to pretend that I am still in the first half of the game, but I am really somewhere in the third quarter. Many Baby Boomers who think that they are in the third quarter are well into overtime.* Needless to say some actuarial tricksters try to cheat the biological realities by leaving childhood out of the calculus. The noted psychologist Erik Erikson, for example, cleverly referred to the period from age 40 to 65 as the "middle adult years," ignoring the fact that a sizable number of people drop dead during this "middle" period. Yet even if one were to exclude the first ten years of human existence from the half-life equation—on the grounds that toddling in diapers is not really "living"—we would still hit our average halfway point in our mid-forties. And one could just as easily lop off the final ten years—on the grounds that doddering in diapers is also not really "living"—which would push our mean half-life back under thirty-five. Any way one crunches the numbers, the period between exiting the university dorms and entering assisted living is objectively more fleeting than it seems subjectively at the outset. If the *average* life expectancy is seventy-seven years and change, half the people out there—and half the readers of this essay—are bound to die younger,

*You have now reached the halfway point of this essay: a cause for either relief or regret. In any case half the author's argument now lies behind you.

often much younger, than that. For every Jeanne Calment, someone must suffer a massive heart attack at fifty or choke to death on a chicken bone at thirty-five.

Life expectancies have increased dramatically over the past century, and human half-lives have lengthened accordingly. When my great-grandparents keeled over in their fifties and sixties, six decades was considered a full life. One of my favorite headlines, from the St. Petersburg *Independent* of September 25, 1930, reads: "Average 1930 Child May Expect to Live until 58 Years of Age." Critics argued Ronald Reagan, at 69, was too old to serve as president. After all, he had already out-distanced Teddy Roosevelt (who died at 60), Woodrow Wilson (67), FDR (63), and LBJ (64)—none of whom had perished young by contemporary standards. As a child, my paternal grandmother—now nearly ninety-one—had hoped to live to seventy. In the 1960s, when my mother's uncle turned eighty, the event was so novel among these first- and second-generation Jewish immigrants that they catered a formal event as lavish as a wedding.

Today many people—if they can remain in good health—aspire to live past ninety or even one hundred. As a physician I would never dream of consoling someone that a relative lived a "full life" at seventy or even eighty. Anything short of eighty-five, in my experience, leaves surviving family members feeling cheated.

What is most troubling about human half-lives is not their brevity, but what is revealed when they are seen in relationship to each other. We may all play by roughly the same statistics, but we are not all operating on the same timetable. By the moment I reach my own half-life, I will almost certainly have used up half of the time I will ever have with my parents, who are in their mid-sixties. Even if my grandmother lives to one hundred, three-quarters of my time with her has already passed. When I have kids of my own, their time remaining with me, as they age, will diminish by the same proportions. This rule explains one of the great mathematical conundrums of my childhood: if at twenty-five a man is half the age of his fifty-year-old father, and at fifty he is two-thirds the age of his dad, at what point in time will the two men be the same age? For those of you who have forgotten your college calculus, the short answer is never.

What happiness one achieves in life derives, at its foundation, from the recognition that a human being is more than just twice a half-life. Some people transcend their mortality raising children, others raising cathedrals and skyscrapers. A few scribble humorous essays, hoping future generations will still find references to the French Foreign Legion mildly amusing. So Mozart lives not three and a half decades, but three and a half centuries. Keats may have died at twenty-six, but a Keats poem remains a joy forever. And that is the miracle that separates us from the morning glories and the mayflies and the uranium: an utterly irrational wish that our contribution will leave the world a better place, even after we no longer remain to reap the benefits. Even if this essay is relegated to the obscurity of college libraries, and then to off-site storage facilities, the potential remains for its rediscovery, or a great twenty-fifth- or thirty-fifth-century renaissance in celebration of its author.

When one includes the possibility of posthumous influence, no human being ever reaches his or her half-life. We remain always on the front nine, always with more coil ahead than behind. We are all approaching our half-life—me as I write this essay, you as you read it. Mercifully it remains forever beyond our reach.

About the author

Jacob M. Appel is a physician, attorney, and bioethicist based in New York City. He is the author of the novel *The Man Who Wouldn't Stand Up,* the short fiction collection *Scouting for the Reaper,* and more than two hundred published stories. He also writes about the nexus of law and medicine, contributing to many leading publications including the *New York Times, San Francisco Chronicle, Boston Globe, Chicago Tribune,* and *Detroit Free Press.* His work has been nominated for the O. Henry Award, Best American Short Stories, Best American Non-required Reading, Best American Essays, and the Pushcart Prize anthology on many occasions.